WILLIAM SEARS, M.D., and MARTHA SEARS, R.N., are the pediatrics experts to whom American parents are increasingly turning for advice and information on all aspects of pregnancy, birth, childcare, and family nutrition. Dr. Sears was trained at Harvard Medical School's Children's Hospital and Toronto's Hospital for Sick Children, the largest children's hospital in the world. He has practiced pediatrics for nearly thirty years and currently serves as a medical and parenting consultant to *Baby Talk* and *Parenting* magazines. Martha Sears is a registered nurse, certified childbirth educator, and breastfeeding consultant. The Searses are the parents of eight children.

More information about the Searses can be found at www.SearsParenting.com and www.AskDrSears.com.

SEARS PARENTING LIBRARY

The Pregnancy Book
The Baby Book
The Birth Book
The Breastfeeding Book
The Fussy Baby Book
The Discipline Book
The Family Nutrition Book
The A.D.D. Book
The Attachment Parenting Book

PARENTING.COM FAQ BOOKS

The First Three Months
How to Get Your Baby to Sleep
Keeping Your Baby Healthy
Feeding the Picky Eater

SEARS CHILDREN'S LIBRARY

Baby on the Way
What Baby Needs

Keeping Your Baby Healthy

America's Foremost Baby and
Childcare Experts Answer the Most
Frequently Asked Questions

William Sears, M.D.,
and Martha Sears, R.N.

Little, Brown and Company

BOSTON | NEW YORK | LONDON

FIRST EDITION

The information herein is not intended to replace the services of trained health professionals. You are advised to consult with your child's health-care professional with regard to matters relating to your child's health, and in particular matters that may require diagnosis or medical attention.

Library of Congress Cataloging-in-Publication Data

Sears, William, M.D.
    Keeping your baby healthy / by William Sears and Martha Sears. — 1st ed.
        p. cm. — (Sears parenting library)
    ISBN 0-316-77680-7
    1. Infants — Care. 2. Infants — Care — Miscellanea. 3. Child care —
Miscellanea. 4. Consumer education. I. Sears, Martha. II. Title.

    RJ61 .S44193 2001
    649'.122 — dc21   00-050695

10 9 8 7 6 5 4 3 2

Printed in the United States of America

Book design and text composition by L&G McRee

Introduction

For years doctors have recognized the therapeutic value of a parent's touch. During my nearly thirty years as a pediatrician, I've grown to greatly respect how much faster children heal when their parents are fully informed about their child's illness or condition and understand their own vital role in helping their child recover.

I tell parents in my pediatrics practice that medical care is a partnership between parents and doctors. Your child depends on you to use preventive measures to help him stay healthy. If he gets sick, your child relies on you to be a trusted member of the medical team to help speed his recovery. Your role is to be a keen observer and an accurate reporter. Your doctor's role is to take the information you observe and report and then make the right diagnosis and prescribe effective treatment—all with the goal of getting your child well again.

In this book I give you my time-tested remedies. You will read about some known and some little-known tips for practicing preventive medicine, such as feeding your child immune-boosting foods, allergy-proofing your child's sleeping environment, "hosing little noses" to keep them clean and infection-free, and a variety of tried-and-true Sears family home remedies that not only reduce the frequency of illnesses but also lessen their severity.

Throughout we give suggestions on how to recognize the onset of common illnesses and when to seek medical attention before these illnesses worsen. You will learn when to call your doctor as well as some safe treatments to give your child while waiting for medical attention.

With the advent of managed care, many parents find they no longer have easy access to medical care. The preventive medicine and self-care information you'll learn in this book will make you a wiser participant in keeping your child healthy.

WILLIAM SEARS, M.D., and MARTHA SEARS, R.N.

Keeping Your Baby Healthy

Jaundice and Newborns

Q *Our pediatrician said my new baby had jaundice and needed to stay in the hospital a few more days. What is jaundice, and why is it dangerous to newborns?*

A Jaundice (also known as hyperbilirubinemia) happens because babies are born with more red blood cells than they need. When the liver breaks down these excess cells, it releases a yellow pigment called bilirubin. The newborn's immature liver can't dispose of bilirubin quickly, and the excess yellow pigment settles in the eyeballs and skin of the newborn, causing a yellow tinge the first week or two. This kind of jaundice, called "physiological jaundice" because it is a normal quirk in a newborn baby's body chemistry, causes no harm to the baby. Once your baby's bilirubin-disposal system matures and the excess red blood cells diminish, the jaundice subsides (usually within a week or two).

In some situations, such as when the mother and baby have different blood types, the bilirubin level goes higher than usual. If this level goes too high for too long, it can cause brain damage. Your doctor will monitor the degree of jaundice through blood samples taken once or twice a day. Besides giving your baby extra fluids to wash out the excess bilirubin, your doctor may recommend placing your baby under a phototherapy lamp or wrapping him in a phototherapy blanket, which dissolves the extra bilirubin pigment in baby's skin, thereby reducing the bilirubin in his blood and allowing it to be excreted in the urine.

In the majority of cases newborn jaundice is a harmless condition and disappears without any treatment. As long as the bilirubin level doesn't stay too high for too long, it should cause no harm to baby or worry to new parents.

🍃

Immunizations and Diabetes

Q *My neighbor's toddler was diagnosed with juvenile diabetes about one month after an immunization shot. Do you think there is a connection between the booster and her illness?*

A There's unlikely to be any connection between an immunization and the development of diabetes. Immunizations have been unfairly blamed for all sorts of illnesses, from attention deficit disorder (A.D.D.) to autism. Millions of children have been receiving immunizations for over fifty years; if there were a connection between immunizations and diabetes, surely it would have been discovered by now.

You can take great comfort in the fact that many serious illnesses have been prevented by immunizations. Do not let this worry prevent you from getting your child the immunizations recommended by your doctor.

A.D.D. and Toddlers

Q *My two-year-old son requires little sleep and is always climbing or running during the day. He pays attention to me when I speak to him, but his activity level really concerns me. Do you think he has attention deficit disorder?*

A   All two-year-olds seem to have a bit of an attention deficit. Don't even think about A.D.D. at this age. Too many older children are unfairly labeled as A.D.D., and certainly two years of age is too young to be labeled. Many two-year-olds are very active and curious; that is how they learn.

By the time your child is two, you will have an idea of his eventual personality. Some toddlers are laid-back. They are content to sit and play for ten- to fifteen-minute stretches and are quiet by nature. Others are on the go constantly. As one photographer father once said to me, "There's no such thing as a still shot of our toddler!"

It sounds like you have an energetic child with an active personality. Active children need plenty of space. Take your child to parks and on outings as much as possible, since active children tend to get into more trouble when kept indoors. A situation in which there are too many active children in too small a space will lead to toy squabbles. If he likes to climb, show him how to climb safely. Buy some big foam-rubber blocks or cushions and let him climb over the pile in the playroom. It's best to supervise the beginning climber, sort of like you would hold a ladder while someone climbs up. You will find safe toddler climbing gyms at infant-product stores.

Active children who are also impulsive by nature can be accident-prone. If your child leaps before looking, darts across the street before checking for cars, and rushes head-long into toys and piles of objects, you may need to teach him to stop and think for a minute. Play a game we call "Rewind" or "Replay." For example, if your impulsive toddler runs toward a puddle of water and slips and falls, replay this impulsive activity. Walk him toward the puddle and stop and look at it. Show him how to walk around it. Teaching a child to think before he acts is a valuable acci-dent-prevention tool that may save your active toddler bumps and bruises later on.

If your child is becoming increasingly impulsive, acting without thinking and becoming more accident-prone, that is cause for concern. This means he needs more supervision, structuring of a safe playing environment, and a bit of hands-on guidance to teach him to think before he acts.

In some active toddlers there is an obvious correlation between how they act and what they eat. If you notice that your child becomes more impulsive and hyperactive after eating junk food, then he may be sugar-sensitive, and de-junking your toddler's diet may help his behavior. Also, some children get hyper after they eat artificial colorings. Rid your child's diet of highly sugared, highly colored soft drinks and packaged foods.

A toddler's behavior also improves with grazing on five or six mini-meals a day instead of three big meals a day. Let him nibble on protein foods (such as yogurt and whole-grain cookies) and complex carbohydrates (such as are found in fruits, vegetables, whole grains, and pasta). Many parents notice that their child's hyperactivity declines following improved nutrition.

✍

Noisy Breather

Q *My two-month-old daughter makes a lot of noise while breathing. She grunts and squeaks and sounds congested. Recent lateral neck and chest X rays were normal. The doctor believes the cause is inflammation of the vocal cords from suctioning her at birth (she had meconium inside before delivery), but I'm still concerned. Do you have any ideas?*

A Two-month-olds are naturally noisy breathers. In fact, pediatricians often refer to this congested stage as the two-month cold. Babies this age produce a great deal of saliva in preparation for teething. Your baby probably produces more saliva than she can swallow, which results in saliva pooling at the back of her throat. Air passing through the puddle of saliva with each breath makes a noise. If your baby's noisy breathing is due simply to this, she'll sound congested but won't experience any discomfort. As long as she feeds and sleeps well, there is no need to worry about the congestion.

On the other hand, your daughter could be allergic to

something in her immediate sleeping environment—probably dust collectors, such as fuzzy toys. Do some detective work to identify and remove dust collectors from the area where she sleeps.

It is also possible, as your doctor believes, that your baby's noisy breathing is caused by an inflammation of the vocal cords that resulted from the suctioning procedure at birth. If this is the case, inhalations will be noticeably noisier than exhalations, and the sound will be consistent with each breath.

If your baby seems to be nasally congested, flush her nose with saltwater nose drops. This solution, available over the counter at your pharmacy, comes in a tiny squirt bottle. You can also make your own nose drops by dissolving a pinch of salt (no more than ¼ teaspoon) in an 8-ounce glass of warm tap water. Use a plastic eyedropper to squirt a few drops into each nostril and gently suction the nose clear using a nasal aspirator. We call this technique "hosing the nose."

Whatever the cause, your baby is likely to outgrow these sound effects within the next couple of months. During that time, she'll learn to swallow her excess saliva, and any vocal-cord inflammation will gradually heal. In the meantime, you will have allergy-proofed her sleeping environment.

Choosing a Fever Medication

Q *My son is a year old and has been sick with a slight fever, runny nose, and cough for several weeks. The doctor told us to alternate Tylenol with Advil or Motrin for the fever at night and to give him regular cold and cough syrup during the day. But I'm confused about the amounts. The directions on the children's bottle of syrup—which seems to be the same product as the more expensive infant drops—do not specify the correct dosage for a one-year-old who weighs 20 pounds. Help!*

A Fever-lowering medications come in many preparations, so figuring out which one to give your baby can be confusing. Acetaminophen (Tylenol) and ibuprofen (Advil, Motrin) come in three formulations: infant drops, syrup (suspension), and chewable tablets. While the drops are easiest to administer, they are the most expensive. Your one-year-old can take the less expensive children's suspension. The suspension is formulated in a concentration of 160 milligrams per teaspoon. Dosage is calculated on a milligram-per-pound basis—7 to 8 milligrams per pound. So the correct dosage for a 20-pound baby would be 1 teaspoonful taken before bedtime or up to four times a day as needed.

Thigh Muscle Pain

Q *My three-and-a-half-year-old son recently woke up with pain in his thigh muscle and walked with difficulty for a few hours. This happened after he had taken a forty-minute walk, which I assumed was the cause of the pain. He was okay for a week, but then he started limping again. The pain does not prevent him from playing or walking, but I am worried that something may be wrong.*

A Any limp that persists should be thoroughly checked out by your child's physician. Most important, your son should have a thorough hip exam. Even though the pain is in his thigh, problems in the hip joint often reveal themselves as pain in the thigh or knee. If not detected and treated, an inflammation of the hip joint could lead to debilitating arthritis of the hip. Though most likely this is simply a harmless quirk of an active child, it is still important to have your child's hip checked out.

Identifying Developmental Problems

Q *We are concerned about our two-and-a-half-year-old son's development. We have noticed that he's easily overwhelmed in a group of kids and often resorts to throwing toys or isolating himself. His language skills are limited to simple commands and phrases, and he flaps his hands and hops in place when excited or overwhelmed. Up until eighteen months he ate almost anything, but now he limits his diet to certain foods. At first I thought he might be autistic, but although he plays with dust motes and finds it difficult to express his thoughts, he clearly wants to communicate with other people. He currently attends preschool, where an aide helps him with daily routines. In a couple of weeks, he'll be evaluated by a team of professionals—a psychologist, physical therapist, speech therapist, pediatrician, and social worker. Are there particular things I should be looking for in this process?*

A We applaud you for following your intuition that your child may be experiencing developmental problems and for seeking professional help. The combination of language delay and aggressive behavior during play certainly merits professional evaluation. You are also wise to have chosen a team approach to evaluate your child. We gather from your comment about his limited diet that he has food sensitivities, which in themselves could cause bizarre behavior (but would not account for the language delay).

You can help the professional team by making a list of

your observations and major concerns about your child's behavior. What you tell the experts may actually be more beneficial to your child's treatment plan than their own observations are.

When assessing your son's speech delay, the evaluators will want to know what your child understands rather than what he says. If your child understands most of what you say, his hearing is probably okay. It's also important to identify what triggers "good" and "bad" behavior and to monitor his language and behavior progression. For example, keep track of the phrases he says at two and a half that he didn't say at two. And note whether the "biggies" (the behaviors you want to shape positively) are getting worse, getting better, or staying the same. This information will help the evaluators determine whether your son is experiencing a normal behavioral and development variance that time and maturity will self-correct or whether he does indeed have a developmental difference that requires specific therapy.

Finally, even with the team approach it's important to remember that parents are the most important therapists and advocates for a child with developmental differences.

ℰ

Baby Heartburn

Q *Our six-week-old son has terrible digestive problems and seems incredibly uncomfortable. Since he appeared a little gassy, we've been feeding him one to two*

drops of Mylicon daily, and ever since, he has been expe-
riencing sporadic choking and even gasping within an
hour of eating. The choking appears out of nowhere and is
sometimes preceded by vomiting, but his temperature
remains normal. He also tends to cry for no apparent
reason. Could he just be getting colicky?

A Most likely your son has a condition called gastro-esophageal reflux (GER). The most common symptoms are spitting up shortly after a feeding, waking up at night in pain, colicky, painful episodes during the day, frequent coughs and colds, and general upset. With GER, the baby regurgitates irritating stomach acids into his esophagus—similar to what adults call heartburn.

Everyone has a band of muscle around his or her esophagus (the tube that runs from the throat to the stomach). This band acts as a valve to keep stomach contents from coming back up. But in some people, this muscle doesn't work very well. As many as one-half of all babies are affected by some degree of reflux, and most of these children do not need medication.

Just to be safe, make an appointment with your doctor specifically for evaluation of GER. An X ray can often diagnose this. Even if the X ray looks normal, your child could still have GER, in which case your doctor will probably want to give your baby an anti-reflux medication. These safe and effective medicines diminish the amount of acid in baby's tummy and help it empty faster.

If your baby's GER doesn't require medication, here are some simple home remedies that you can use:

- Keep your baby upright for at least thirty minutes after each feeding.
- Offer smaller, more frequent feedings.

- Burp your baby well during and after each feeding.
- If you are using formula, experiment with different formulas, such as a soy formula or a hypoallergenic formula (Alimentum or Nutramigen). Allergy to formula can also contribute to your baby's symptoms.
- Elevate the head of your baby's crib 30 degrees. A reflux wedge, available at any infant-product store, will make this easier, or try Crib Blox, which will fit under the crib's legs.
- Wear your baby in a baby sling as much as possible to minimize crying (babies experience more reflux while crying). Several mothers in our practice have found that their infants' GER diminished after being worn in a sling for several hours a day. The reason, they believe, is that babywearing after feeding promotes digestive organization. Gentle motion and closeness to mother seem to enhance intestinal function. Perhaps this is similar to the effect produced when a mother cat licks her kittens' abdomens after feeding.

One hidden cause of digestive problems in newborns is sensitivity to something in mother's milk (such as wheat or dairy). Breastfeeding moms can do a little detective work to try to figure out which foods need to be eliminated from their diet, starting with the most common culprits, dairy products. If after a week there is no improvement, other foods may have to be eliminated. Our book *The Fussy Baby Book* (Little, Brown, 1996) contains more detailed information about babies with digestive upsets or colic. We include a step-by-step approach to diagnosis and treatment and instructions on how a mom can eliminate foods from her diet that may be upsetting her baby's tummy.

Most babies outgrow their reflux by seven to eight months, mainly because they spend much of their day upright, taking advantage of gravity to hold food and milk in their stomachs.

☙

Lazy Eye

Q *My three-year-old daughter was diagnosed with lazy eye. She told the doctor her "left eye was very sad because it could not see," but her "right eye was happy because it could see." The doctor said diagnosing lazy eye in preschoolers is rare and we are very lucky that treatment can be started. What is lazy eye? Is it common? How is it treated?*

A Lazy eye, also called amblyopia, is defined as poor vision in one eye. It has three major causes: misaligned or crossed eyes (a condition known as strabismus); unequal focus in the two eyes; and cloudiness in the eye tissues.

The most obvious form of lazy eye is strabismus. Normally, both eyes work together so that when one muscle group pulls an eye to one side, the corresponding muscles in the other eye reciprocate, resulting in both eyes moving together in perfect harmony. If one eye moves to the side but the other eye doesn't, the child's vision will be blurry, and often the child will "see double."

It's very important to detect strabismus early in a child's development. Failure to detect a lazy eye muscle early on can result in diminished vision in the affected eye. There are some types of lazy eye that you don't need to worry about, and no treatment is necessary. Sometimes the lazy eye deviates only occasionally, such as when the child is tired, upset, or when a child willingly makes her eyes cross. This occasional lazy eye usually self-corrects. Even so, your child should frequently be examined by an eye doctor to make sure it's not getting worse.

Persistent strabismus, on the other hand, should be corrected either by glasses or surgery. Wearing glasses for a year or two can often correct a mild weakness and strengthen the muscles in the weak eye. Your child's eye doctor will periodically examine your child's eyes to be sure the muscles are strengthening. Sometimes muscle weakness needs to be corrected by surgery. Oftentimes, an eye doctor will first recommend that your child wear glasses for a trial period before recommending surgery.

Sometimes a child's eyes may look crossed but really not be. Children with a wide nasal bridge or prominent folds of skin in the nasal corner of the eyes can look cross-eyed when they really aren't. This condition is called pseudo-strabismus.

Here's how to tell if your child's eyes are really crossed. Get used to looking at your child's eyes when they appear straight. Shine a flashlight toward her eyes. Or take a photograph of the child's eyes. Notice the pinpoint reflection of the flashlight or the flash in the photograph. The white dot should be in the same place in each eye. Using a baseball-diamond analogy, if the dot is at the pitcher's mound in one eye and at first or third base in the other eye, your child's eyes are crossed. If the dots are at the pitcher's mound or at the same base in both eyes, they are not crossed.

If you're wondering whether or not your child's eyes are crossed, it's always best to have them checked by a pediatric eye specialist. Early detection and treatment increases your child's chances of eventually having good vision.

☙

Treating an Itchy Rash

Q *My son developed a thick, itchy rash on his wrists and behind his knees that was diagnosed as eczema by our allergist. He was given a prescription for a steroid cream, but after several weeks the rash is still there. Is there another treatment that does not involve steroids?*

A The itchy rash on your child's wrists and legs does sound like eczema, and usually a steroid cream will clear it up. Eczema is dry, patchy, itchy, scaly skin, either caused by an allergy to food or to something touched, or it can be the nonallergic type that is an inherited trait. The medical term for eczema is atopic dermatitis. Eczema appears most commonly on the cheeks, behind the knees, in the skin folds of the arms, and in the groin.

Sometimes an area of skin itches intensely before a rash is even visible. In fact, eczema is often referred to as an itch that rashes. This skin condition is most common in infancy and the preschool years and tends to improve with time. It usually flares up in the winter months because of the skin-drying effects of central heating and is aggravated by sweating, strong soaps, stress, and exposure to certain fabrics.

The first line of treatment is to figure out the cause. The

most common eczema-producing allergens are soaps, detergents, fabrics (especially wool), foods (eggs, dairy, and wheat), and carpet fibers. Stress may also precipitate eczema. In that case, any measures that will make the environment less stressful should relieve the eczema.

Itching is the most intense discomfort of eczema, and scratching only causes more irritation and rash, which in turn causes more itching. Therefore, over time, the itch-scratch cycle produces thickened skin. Sometimes the scratching breaks down the protective layer of outer skin and allows a bacterial infection to develop (recognized by puslike, yellow, crusty, weeping drainage). To relieve the itching, try the following:

- Keep a cool, humid environment. Use a vaporizer or humidifier in your child's bedroom. The dry air of central heating aggravates eczema.
- Use soap sparingly—only once or twice a week—since it is drying to the skin. Try a creamy, gentle soap, such as Dove, Neutrogena, or Cetaphil cleanser.
- Apply an emollient, such as Soothe and Heal with Lansinoh or Aquaphor Healing Ointment, before bedtime, as a lubricant dressing to cover your child's eczema.
- Cut your child's fingernails short to minimize scratching.
- Try cool, nonsoapy baths to reduce the itching. Add oatmeal or Aveeno as a soothing compound (1 cup per tub).
- Avoid long soaks in the tub, since excessive exposure to water robs the skin of its natural oils. Brief showers are better.
- Rinse your child thoroughly after he's been swimming in a chlorinated pool.
- Dress your child in loose, breathable cotton clothing.

- Try steroid creams. These are usually very effective in the treatment of eczema but should be used only as directed by your doctor and only when the eczema is severe and not helped by the above simpler measures. Using too strong a cream too often can permanently discolor the skin.

The best treatment for eczema is from the inside and the outside. The above treatments are aimed at the outside. To treat chronic, scaly, dry skin from the inside, increase the amount of omega-3 dietary fats. The best sources are coldwater fish (salmon and tuna), canola oil, and flax oil. If your child will not take any of these dietary sources of omega 3, try Neuromins capsules, a natural DHA omega-3 supplement made from seaweed. Neuromins capsules are available at most nutrition stores. To find your nearest source of Neuromins, call the manufacturer at 800-OKBRAIN.

In our pediatrics practice, we have seen amazing results simply by adding increased dietary omega 3's to the above measures. The good news is that eczema improves with time. The earlier you start this prevention regimen, the healthier your child's skin will be.

℘

Children and Depression

Q *Depression runs in my husband's family. There are days when my three-year-old mopes around and doesn't*

*want to play with her toys or friends. I think she may be
depressed. Should I have her evaluated? How do you know
if a child is depressed?*

A You are wise in considering depression as a cause of
your child's inactivity. Childhood depression is one of the
most frequently missed problems because we don't tend to
think of children as getting depressed. Consider other possibilities as well, however. Some children are quiet by
nature. They are content to sit and play by themselves. But
if your child mopes around with a sad face, some professional and parental help is in order.

If the things that make most children happy, such as
going to a movie, having a party, or buying a toy or dress,
don't work with your child, your child may be depressed.
Eyes mirror a child's mind. If most of the time she doesn't
have a happy, sparkly look, she may be depressed. Also,
depressed children often have dry skin, suffer from constipation, tend to be overweight or underweight, and generally have poor eating habits. Here is a bit of home therapy
you might try:

- *Model happiness.* Take inventory of what messages all
  family members are reflecting to your child. Do you
  reflect happiness or sadness? Put on a happy face in
  front of your child as much as possible.
- *Take a total family inventory.* Are there family situations
  that cause your child to be down, such as a move, mar-
  ital discord, a new sibling, sibling squabbles, or a new
  day care? Catch your child in a verbal mood and
  encourage her to ventilate her feelings. You'll be sur-
  prised how candid a three-year-old can be.
- *Discover your child's special talent.* What is one activity
  she especially likes to do? Spend a lot of time with her

doing that special something. Enjoying one activity and excelling at it can become a general mood elevator to get her going into other activities. Find out what she likes to do best and get her involved with this.

* *Be the social chairman to jump-start your unmotivated child.* Invite personality-compatible friends over to your home.
* *Watch what she eats.* There is growing research showing the connection between what children eat and how they feel. The biochemical basis of this food-mood relationship is neurotransmitters, those chemical messengers that relay thought and actions along the trillions of neuropathways in the brain. Some children—we call them "vulnerable kids"—are very sensitive to junk foods in their diets. Some foods are "happy foods"; other foods are "sad foods." Mood foods vary from child to child, so keep track of which foods seem to perk your child up and which foods cause her to feel down.

Many basically happy children go through down periods, a sort of "funk" in which they are unmotivated to do anything. They need periodic parental perk-ups to get them going again. Keep a diary and chart your child's moods. What situations trigger happy behavior? Which situations trigger sad moods? If you find your child has periodic down periods, try to identify the trigger. If you find your child's down periods are becoming more frequent and lasting longer than the up periods, seek professional counseling for your child.

༂

Testosterone and Preschoolers

Q *I read that preschoolers get a burst of testosterone at age three or four that causes their new aggressiveness and anger. Is this true?*

A Aggressive behavior in men is often blamed on testosterone. There is some biological truth to the hormone-behavior connection. With that said, you don't have to put up with annoying behavior just because of a child's gender. Here are some ways to tame the aggressor:

• *Model nonaggression.* A child who lives with aggression becomes aggressive. Preschool children often pick up aggressive behavior from older siblings. If young children see older ones hitting, pushing, or yelling at each other, they'll think that aggressive behavior is a normal way of life. Remember, preschoolers are searching for what is the norm and will model the behavior they see. If this is happening in your home, teach the older children the exact behavior you want them to model for the younger ones. Preschoolers pick up behavior from their peers. Perhaps your child has gotten into the wrong crowd. Do a site visit to his day care or preschool and see if he is around a lot of aggressive children and if his behaviors remain unsupervised and unchecked. You may need to make a change in play groups, day care, or preschool.

Some impulsive children act before they think. Help your child control these impulses by "thinking first" or "counting to three" before flying off the handle. This teaches self-control. You can also help your child overcome aggressive impulses by showing him substitute behaviors that he can click into at the first thought of aggression. For example, say, "As soon as you feel like hitting, grab a pillow and pound it. Or go run around the yard," or, "Next time you feel like hitting, grab your hand and talk to it: 'Now, hand, you should not hit people.'" He'll also see the humor in this.

- *Mellow the mean streaks.* A child who habitually bangs toys, bashes dolls, mistreats animals, and pounds on walls is sending up a red flag. Besides delving into the roots of his anger, encourage more gentle play: "Hug the teddy bear," "Pet the kitty," "Love the doll." Construct a reward chart. "Every day you are nice to your friends, we'll put a happy face on the chart, and after three happy faces we'll have a special treat."

- *Supervise the aggressor.* It's neither fair nor safe to allow aggressive children to play with potential victims without a parent on watch. If your child is aggressive, share your concern with the other parents and teachers in the play group, and seek their help in tempering your child's aggressive behavior. Don't hesitate to tell them about the problem, and encourage them to step in. They may also have struggled through an aggressive stage with their own children. Your candidness shows your concern for their children. Otherwise, aggressive behavior in your child may come between your friendships with other parents. Be careful, though, not to give the aggressor too much attention that sets him apart from other children in the play group.

- *Show and tell your child how to act in a group.* Give him substitute behaviors: "We don't hit, we hug," as you show a hitting child how to hug the other child. If your

child is going through a physical stage, let him act out
his physical needs by "give me five" hand-slapping
games rather than hitting people.

- *Give consequences that your child can understand.* "If
you hit, you must sit." Give a time-out to the aggressor.
This is a temporary break in the action when the child
has time to reflect on how he should have acted. Keep a
diary of what triggers aggressive behavior. Is he tired?
Bored? Hungry? Are there too many children in too
small a space? Oftentimes identifying and removing the
trigger sets your child up for less aggressive play.

Above all, don't fall into the trap of the "ignore it, he'll
grow out of it" advice. Ignoring any undesirable behavior
deprives a child of the social tools to succeed in life and
deprives you of finding creative discipline strategies.

✍

Roseola: The Three-Day Fever

Q *My son, who just turned one, has had a 101° F fever
for about three days. We went to the doctor yesterday and
found out that he does not have an ear infection. He got
over bronchitis about two weeks ago, but he's not
wheezing now. What else could it be?*

A The most common cause of a three-day febrile illness in a child between nine and eighteen months of age is
roseola, a nonserious virus characterized by three days of

up-and-down fever. The fever breaks around the fourth day, and a faint pink rash appears, primarily over the chest, abdomen, and extremities.

Roseola is one of the only childhood viral infections in which the rash appears after the fever breaks. In most cases, a baby with roseola doesn't seem that sick by the time the fever is down. You can usually rest assured that baby's illness is over once the rash appears.

Even in the presence of fever, a wise physician does not prescribe an antibiotic without determining a definite reason to do so. In this case if he had, the rash that followed the fever might have been mistaken as an allergic reaction to the antibiotic.

✍

Periorbital Cellulitis

Q *My daughter was recently diagnosed with periorbital cellulitis, which the doctor said was more serious than conjunctivitis. She was put on an antibiotic, but he didn't give me any information about this problem. I would appreciate any information you could provide.*

A Periorbital cellulitis is an infection that spreads around the eyeball. Unlike conjunctivitis, which is simply an inflammation of the white part of the eye, periorbital cellulitis is potentially serious because it can spread behind the eyeball and into the brain.

Depending on the severity of this type of eye infection,

your doctor will give your child either an oral antibiotic or, if it worsens, an injection. If the infection is treated early and properly, your daughter should recover with no after-effects. However, if she develops a high fever, lethargy, and increased swelling and tenderness around the eye and seems to be getting sicker, be sure to notify your doctor; sometimes intravenous antibiotics are necessary.

Breaking Troublesome Habits

Q *My four-year-old daughter has a habit of pulling out her eyelashes. This started when she was three and entered preschool. She is an only child and gets bored at times, but she's doing wonderfully in school and is very active and cheerful. We try to keep her busy, but it's hard to watch her constantly. I'm apprehensive about counseling because it could make her feel like there's really something wrong with her.*

A   As children get older, they often develop annoying habits. Some of these habits go away without parental intervention; others need to be broken before they become mannerisms that lead to unflattering disfigurements or labels.

In breaking annoying habits, the usual parental dilemma is whether or not to confront the child. If the habit is a "biggie" that physically or socially harms the child, it's important to intervene. A "smallie," however, is best ignored. Eyelash pulling is probably a biggie.

Here are steps to help your daughter break her eyelash-pulling habit:

- *Identify the trigger.* Under what conditions does your child pull out her eyelashes? Is she bored, tired, angry, or nervous? Keep a diary to help correlate the eyelash pulling with an identifiable situation. Once you identify the trigger, you can focus on changing the conditions that prompt the habit.
- *Motivate your child to break the habit.* For example, compliment her on her pretty eyelashes and explain why it's best not to pull them out.
- *Suggest a harmless alternative behavior.* Many children develop habits like twitching, nail biting, or hair pulling when they're bored or as temporary distractions from stressful situations. Suggest other ways your daughter can relax besides pulling at her eyelashes. For example, say, "As soon as you feel like you need to pull out your eyelashes, take a deep breath and think about your favorite thing." Or, "When you feel your hand going toward your eyelashes, clasp your hands and squeeze them tight." Give the alternative habit a name, such as "the sub" (for substitute). Then, when your daughter reaches for her eyelashes, quietly remind her, "Remember your sub."

You are right to be hesitant about seeking counseling for your daughter's habit. Going to a professional counselor will convey to your child that her eyelash pulling is a big deal, and this in itself could make her self-conscious. Often it's better for habit-breaking advice to come from a caring parent than from a professional counselor.

Finally, try not to take your daughter's eyelash pulling personally and worry that there may be some underlying stress that you're responsible for detecting and relieving. Simply be there for her, encourage her to understand why she wants to pull out her eyelashes, and help her to ease herself out of this habit.

⚜

Zinc: A Boost to the Immune System

Q *I read about a recent study that said that daily zinc supplements might reduce respiratory infections in preschoolers. The article also said that zinc could help prevent diarrhea and provide protection from illness. Should I give my eighteen-month-old a daily supplement?*

A The study that you're referring to was published in *Pediatrics*, the scientific journal of the American Academy of Pediatrics. Researchers from Johns Hopkins School of Public Health in Baltimore and the All-India Institute of Medical Science in New Delhi, India, evaluated the effect of zinc supplementation on 298 infants and children aged six months to thirty-five months and compared them with a nonsupplemented group of about the same size. The infants in the supplemented group received a daily dose of 10 milligrams of zinc for six months.

At the end of the study, the supplemented group had higher concentrations of zinc in their blood than did the nonsupplemented group, and they experienced half the number of respiratory infections. The authors concluded that zinc supplementation, at least in the study group, could lower the incidence of acute lower-respiratory infections in preschoolers by as much as 45 percent.

The children enrolled in this study were from a low socioeconomic population of urban India and not well nourished. However, even reasonably nourished suburban American children could probably benefit from zinc supplements. Children under a year get zinc in formula or from breast milk, so they don't need additional zinc. Previous research has shown that zinc also helps mobilize infection-fighting white blood cells by aiding them in releasing antibodies.

To make sure your child is getting enough zinc, feed her zinc-rich food or give her a daily supplement of 10 milligrams. There are quite a few foods that supply beneficial amounts of zinc for your child. Zinc-fortified cereals can contain up to 15 milligrams of zinc per ounce, but be sure to check the label. Three ounces of crab contain 7 milligrams of zinc; 3 ounces of beef contain 6 milligrams; and ½ cup of beans contains 1.2 to 1.8 milligrams.

Zinc supplements are available in capsules and lozenges. You can entice your toddler to take the supplement by hiding a capsule in a spoonful of yogurt or sprinkling its contents over cereal. Be careful not to exceed the recommended daily dose. More is not necessarily better or safer. In some cases excess minerals or vitamins can lead to health problems.

In addition to zinc, try these other immune-boosters:

• *Serve foods rich in antioxidants.* Antioxidants help control free-radical molecules that can attack healthy cells. In research, free radicals have been shown to disrupt and tear apart vital cell structures, such as cell membranes.

Antioxidants have been shown to tie up these free radicals and take away their destructive power—perhaps
reducing some chronic diseases. Antioxidants include
vitamin C (found in oranges, grapefruits, mangos, tomatoes, broccoli, spinach, peppers, and kale); vitamin E
(found in seeds, nuts, grains, and vegetable oils); and
carotenoids, such as beta carotene (found in leafy green
vegetables, yellow vegetables, and yellow fruits,
including cantaloupe, apricots, peaches, carrots, broccoli, collard greens, spinach, kale, sweet potatoes, and
yams).

* *Monitor your child's sugar intake.* Research on adults
  has shown that eating or drinking 100 grams (3 ounces)
  or more of sugar (the amount in most cans of soda)
  during one meal can depress the immune system by
  reducing the white blood cells' ability to fight germs.

* *Encourage your child to eat a nutritious diet and to
  exercise.* Diet and exercise will help him avoid the dan-
  gers of excess fat. Obesity can lead to a depressed
  immune system by affecting the white blood cells'
  ability to multiply and produce antibodies.

* *Protect your child from or help her deal with stressful
  situations.* Stress taxes the immune system by producing
  hormones that reduce the number of white blood cells
  that circulate throughout the body. This is why adults
  and children often get sick during or after a stressful situation.

* *Plan meals that contain a mix of different-colored foods.*
  By doing this you can often ensure that your child
  receives a combination of the food groups, as well as
  infection-fighting foods. But this isn't groundbreaking
  advice. Our grandmothers advocated balanced meals as
  a route to good health long before the sophisticated
  research methods of today proved them right.

🐦

Vitamin Supplements for Breastfed Babies

Q *My baby is two months old. Our pediatrician told me to start giving her vitamin drops with iron when she was a month old. But when I try giving her the drops, she spits them up. I've read that a breastfed baby gets enough nutrients from her mother's milk, at least until she is six months old. Is this true? If not, how can I successfully give her the drops? Can I wait until she's four months old and stir the drops into her cereal, or will that make them less effective?*

A Mother Nature provides all the necessary nutrients a baby needs in mother's milk, so a healthy full-term baby who is getting enough breast milk does not need iron or vitamin supplements.

The custom of giving these supplements to babies is based upon outdated information. Decades ago, when the nutritional content of breast milk was analyzed, it was found (on paper) to be low in iron and some vitamins. However, new information shows that even though the iron and vitamins in breast milk may be lower in quantity, they are superior in quality. These nutrients enjoy a higher bioavailability, meaning that more of the iron—and probably more of the vitamins—are better absorbed in mother's milk than those added to commercial formulas or cereal.

If your baby was premature, had a low birth weight, or

does not seem to be getting enough breast milk, your doctor may recommend nutritional supplements. If your doctor is worried about your baby's iron stores, he or she may check your baby's hemoglobin, usually at your baby's nine-month checkup. But for the first six months, have confidence that your milk can provide all the nutrition your baby needs.

❧

Diagnosing Vomiting and Fever

Q *Last Saturday my five-month-old daughter started vomiting everything I fed her. By Sunday she was running a low-grade fever. I saw the pediatrician Monday and was told she just had a virus. But the vomiting has continued for five days, and her temperature is still 100° F. I'm worried that something else is wrong and my doctor just doesn't see it. Even Tylenol won't lower her temperature. Help! Am I missing something?*

A You may have cause to worry. Most viral infections go away by five days; some take seven. Always follow your intuition. If your maternal instinct tells you something more is going on than just a viral infection, tell your doctor.

Pediatrics is a partnership between you and your doctor. Your job is to watch for signs and symptoms, paying special attention to how your baby's condition changes. Your doctor's job is to figure out why your baby is sick. Doctors rely heavily on parents' observations and intuitions. If you feel something more is going on, that is often the case.

Anytime a little girl has a "fever of unknown origin," while it's usually a virus that will go away on its own, it could be a urinary tract infection. Take your baby back to your doctor and ask the nurse to put a urine-collecting bag on your baby. Often the signs of an infection may not be easy to spot early on. Whenever your baby's condition doesn't follow the path predicted by your doctor, take her back for reexamination. Sometimes a throat, ear, chest, or urine infection is not apparent early in the course of the illness.

It sounds as though your baby is not taking enough fluids, which will only prolong the fever. To keep her from getting dehydrated, give her small, frequent feedings and an oral rehydration solution, such as Pedialyte. You might try feeding her half as much twice as often.

Thrush and Other Fungal Infections

Q *My son was born with Listeria meningitis and spent twenty-one days in the hospital on antibiotics. He is doing fine now and doesn't seem to have any existing problems as a result of the infection. But when he was three months we noticed whiteness on his tongue, which his doctor identified as thrush. Could my baby have had the thrush ever*

*since he was taken off the antibiotics? And is he likely to
encounter other infections or illnesses as a result of his
medical history?*

A You are fortunate that the meningitis was caught
early and treated properly and that you now have a normal,
healthy baby. The antibiotics used to treat newborn meningitis need to be strong to treat the germs in the spinal fluid.
These same antibiotics also kill the normal bacteria that
inhabit the lining of the intestinal tract, beginning with the
mouth.

Normally, the mouth and intestinal tract are coated with
healthy bacteria that, in return for a warm place to live,
contribute to the health of your baby's intestinal tract,
manufacture vitamins, and battle harmful bacteria. The
antibiotics your son received as an infant threw off this
natural balance between helpful and harmful germs that
line the intestinal tract, allowing the overgrowth of a
fungus (or yeast) called thrush.

Thrush won't harm your baby, but it's a nuisance to
deal with. If you are breastfeeding, you may also get this
fungus on your nipples (your nipples will redden and
you'll experience intense burning and itching). If this happens, put the thrush medicine your doctor prescribes for
your baby on your nipples several times a day.

Thrush is treated with prescription antifungal drops
given three times a day for at least ten days. Paint the
thrush medicine on your baby's tongue and all over the
inside of his mouth, as your doctor prescribes. If you are
formula feeding, it's helpful to mix 1 teaspoon of acidophilus powder in the bottle of formula once a day to
enhance the growth of healthy nutrients and inhibit the
growth of yeast. Acidophilus is one of the healthy, intestinal residents that is killed by the antibiotic. If you are

breastfeeding, mix it in a little water and administer it with a cup throughout the day.

Secondary to the thrush, you may also notice a fungus-type diaper rash that appears as a raised red ring around your baby's anus. An over-the-counter antifungal cream (Lotrimin) applied twice a day for a week should relieve this rash, but it may take several weeks for the thrush to disappear. Regular diaper-rash cream (such as Desitin) will not heal this type of rash. After that, there is no reason why your infant should be more susceptible than any other infant to fungus infections.

⅋

A Knot on Baby's Spine

Q *My daughter is almost eight months old and has a knot on the lower part of her spine. The knot has been there since birth and keeps growing with her. Should I be worried?*

A Any growing knot along the spinal column should be thoroughly evaluated by your baby's doctor. Most of these growths are hemangiomas, which are tissues containing lots of blood vessels that grow with the child. Hemangiomas can occur anywhere on the body and are not malignant. In most cases they gradually disappear between two and three years of age.

Sometimes, however, a hemangioma is hooked to the spinal cord. This is known as a tethered cord. To see if this is the case with your baby, your doctor may recommend a special type of X ray called an MRI. If your daughter's hemangioma extends onto the spinal cord, it must be surgically removed to keep it from interfering with spinal-cord growth. If the growth is not attached to the cord, however, it will not bother her, and your doctor will probably recommend leaving it alone.

℘

Treating Chronic Sinusitis

Q *Our eighteen-month-old baby has chronic sinusitis. Our pediatrician recommended having her adenoids removed. Should we keep her under treatment until she gets older or schedule surgery now?*

A Before submitting your infant to surgery, we suggest that you get an opinion from a pediatric ear, nose, and throat (ENT) specialist. Removing the adenoids because of chronic sinusitis is an unusual form of treatment for a baby at this age. The main reason for removing the tonsils and/or adenoids is sleep apnea, a condition in which the tonsils or adenoids are so large that they obstruct a baby's breathing during sleep. You can recognize sleep apnea by observing your baby's breathing patterns (breathing is fast and noisy, followed by periodic ten- to fifteen-second pauses).

In our experience, if the adenoids are large enough to block sinus drainage, they will also obstruct baby's breathing, especially during sleep. We suggest that you make a tape-recording of your baby's sleep noises. An ENT specialist can diagnose sleep apnea just by listening to the recording. If your baby doesn't have obstructive tonsils or adenoids, consider other treatments for the chronic sinusitis before surgery.

Is your baby primarily a mouth breather or nose breather? If she breathes predominantly through her mouth while awake or asleep, her adenoids are probably blocking airflow and nasal drainage. If she is primarily a nose breather, especially during sleep, it's unlikely that enlarged adenoids are the cause of your child's chronic sinusitis.

Allergies (inhalant or dietary) are the most common cause of recurrent sinus infections in a child at this age. Allergens trigger fluid buildup in the nose and sinuses. The fluid acts as a culture medium for bacteria, resulting in chronic sinusitis.

Here are ways to reduce discomfort caused by allergens:

- *Allergy-proof your baby's bedroom.* Remove dust collectors, such as down comforters and fuzzy toys.
- *Clear the air.* Run a HEPA-type air filter in your baby's room to get rid of pet dander and dust mites. HEPA filters are efficient in filtering out almost 100 percent of airborne allergens and danders and are available at most allergy-supply centers.
- *Banish cigarette smoke.* This is a major cause of chronic sinusitis.
- *Keep her nose clear.* The nose is the entry point for germs and secretions into the sinuses. Try a daily ritual of "hosing the nose." Each time your baby's nose is stuffy, flush it out with a saltwater nasal spray, available over the counter or in a homemade remedy (see page 8).

After the flushing, remove nasal secretions with a nasal aspirator (a gadget veteran parents call a "snot snatcher").

- *Observe other triggers.* Does your baby's nose run or does she sneeze around family pets? If so, eliminate contact with the pet, or at least keep the pet out of baby's room.

ᴥ

Croup

Q *My eight-month-old baby has quite a cough. How do I know if it's croup? And if it is, should she see the doctor?*

A Croup is what doctors call a particular kind of infant cough that sounds a lot like a barking seal. This condition usually starts out as a simple cold and cough, and then it develops into the loud barking cough. Most croupy coughs are caused by a virus and will usually subside within a few days. The best treatment is extra fluids, humidity, and a lot of tender loving care.

There are two types of croup. The first, and more common, version is no more serious than the common cold. The second is a medical emergency demanding immediate care. In determining which variety your baby has, pay attention to her behavior more than the volume of her cough. If your barking baby remains happy and playful, if she is able to sleep without being awakened by her cough, and if her breathing isn't labored and hasn't been compromised in any way, then you don't have anything to worry about.

What makes croup potentially dangerous is the way it inflames an infant's vocal cords, which are inconveniently located in the narrowest part of your baby's airway. The cords sometimes swell enough to obstruct an infant's breathing. Look for these warning signs:

- *A troubled baby.* A baby whose breathing is hampered by a narrowed airway will have a worried look on her face. She will seem panicky and won't want to play or interact. All of her energy will be focused on getting enough air, and she won't lie down or sleep. She'll just sit up and bark.
- *Indrawing and stridor.* Watch the dent in your baby's neck just above her breastbone to see if it caves in with each breath. This is called indrawing. Stridor occurs when a baby's vocal cords swell and narrow her airway to the point where each breath produces a prolonged, almost musical whistling. Both indrawing and stridor are signs that your baby's airway has narrowed and that she has to work to get air. If she is still happy and not distressed by the lack of air, don't worry.

While it's safer to see a doctor immediately if your baby is showing signs of indrawing or stridor, you can ease your baby's discomfort and help her breathe by keeping her relaxed. Keeping your baby calm will help keep her vocal cords relaxed, leaving more room for air to pass through. You'll need to keep yourself calm as well. Seeing you get upset will only make your baby anxious. Sit your baby upright on your lap, play soft music, sing lullabies, read a story, or let her watch a soothing television show. If you are nursing, offer her a breast, the world's best comforter.

Next, humidifying the air softens the crusty secretions that have accumulated on the inflamed vocal cords and allows air to pass through more easily. Take your baby into the bathroom, close the door, turn on a hot shower, and sit on the counter or toilet seat while you hold your baby and read a story, or let her lie with her head on a pillow. Sit with baby on your lap or put her down to sleep with a jet of vaporizer steam directly over her nose. Sleep is one of the best therapies for croup. If you can get your baby to sleep easily, don't worry.

When to Seek Medical Treatment

Rush your baby to the emergency room if she exhibits any of these signs:

- Her indrawing becomes progressively more labored (the little dent above her breastbone deepens further and further as she breathes). Worse, the sound of her breathing gets more and more faint as her indrawing becomes more severe.
- She appears to be struggling to get air.
- She can't speak or cry for lack of breath.
- She is losing her color and becoming more and more anxious.

If weather permits, leave the car windows open for the humidity and ventilation on the way to the emergency room and try to settle your baby with calming sounds, such as her favorite music. Many infants with severe croup improve considerably on the trip to the hospital, simply by getting outside into more humid air.

Common Sense on Sudden Infant Death Syndrome (SIDS)

Q *Reading the latest news about SIDS, I don't know whether to be excited or scared. If the Italian researchers are right, a newborn heart test may indicate whether my baby has a higher chance of dying from SIDS. What can you tell me about this new research? Should I have my baby tested? And what do I do if she's in the higher-risk group? I've also heard that putting her to sleep on her back will protect her. Is this true?*

A Sudden Infant Death Syndrome (SIDS), also known as crib death, is the unexplained death of an infant under one year of age, usually occurring between two and six months. It is usually caused by a defect in the automatic control of breathing during sleep. It's important to note that even though SIDS is high on the list of parents' worries, it is uncommon, occurring in approximately one in one thousand infants.

The Italian research you refer to, published in *The New England Journal of Medicine,* indicated that a specific abnormality in a newborn's electrocardiogram could be a sign that the child is at a higher than average risk for Sudden Infant Death Syndrome. My concern about the screening test mentioned in the study is that it may cause unnecessary anxiety in parents. Also, this research is only a first study, and it needs to be confirmed by other investigations. In the long history of SIDS research, many studies have received a lot of publicity only to be disproven years later.

As the authors of the study suggested, electrocardiograph screening (a test that records the heart's electrical activity) could be effective on infants considered to be at high risk for SIDS. These include siblings of previous SIDS infants (although new insights show that these infants may not be at such a high risk), premature infants who have shown stop-breathing episodes (apnea) while being monitored, or infants of drug-abusing mothers. In the meantime, parents would be wise to take the following steps, which have been proven to lower the risk of SIDS:

- Put your baby to sleep on her back.
- Breastfeed your baby.
- Provide a safe sleeping environment, using a firm mattress and keeping the area free of plush toys or pillows.
- Don't smoke around your baby, before or after birth.

For a more in-depth discussion of understanding and reducing the risk of SIDS, see my book *SIDS: A Parent's Guide to Understanding and Preventing Sudden Infant Death Syndrome* (Little, Brown, 1996).

A Baby's Raised Soft Spot

Q *My son is nine weeks old, and his soft spot still feels a little raised. Is this normal? He has a slight cold but no fever or any other signs of sickness.*

A The soft spot, also called the fontanel, is an open area that provides room for an infant's growing brain. Located near the front of the head at the point where four major skull bones come together, the soft spot gradually becomes smaller until it closes by two years of age. While the area feels soft, it is actually covered by a thick, fibrous membrane, which isn't easily injured. Usually, the soft spot is flat or slightly raised. It is completely normal for the soft spot to be slightly raised, especially during the first nine months. Sometimes you can even see the soft spot pulsate.

It is difficult from your description to tell whether your baby's soft spot is a cause for concern. Run your hand over the top of his head; if you feel a distinct bump, call your doctor. There may be nothing wrong, but a bulging fontanel can signal internal pressure. If the area is not only bulging but also firm, your doctor may order an X ray called a CAT scan.

Sometimes a bulging fontanel is a sign of meningitis. However, if your baby had this illness he would have other severe symptoms as well (such as a high fever, lethargy, and vomiting) that would have already prompted a visit to the doctor.

If the soft spot is sunken and accompanied by vomiting or diarrhea, abdominal pain, decreased urination, dry mouth, and no tears, you should call the doctor. Your baby could be suffering from dehydration.

✑

The Rubella Vaccine

Q *My wife wants to wait until our daughter is eighteen months before giving her the rubella vaccine, because she heard that the vaccine is linked to autism at one year. Is this true? What are the risks of giving the vaccine now versus waiting until eighteen months?*

A To our knowledge there is no proven link between the rubella vaccine and autism or any other behavioral problems. All immunizations have at one time or another been blamed for a behavioral or medical problem, but research usually fails to show any correlation. Rubella, or German measles, is a mild viral illness that does not harm your child. In fact, it is so mild that it is often overlooked.

The main reason to give your daughter the rubella vaccine is to protect her against the germ if she becomes pregnant. When a woman who isn't immune to rubella contracts the virus during pregnancy, the fetus can suffer deformities of the heart, brain, and skin.

Medically speaking, it is unnecessary for a child to have the rubella vaccine until she is fertile. In fact, some countries wait to administer the vaccine until the teen years. The rationale in the United States for using the rubella vaccine in infants (and one we agree with) is that giving every infant a rubella vaccine will eventually eradicate the disease, as the worldwide vaccination program did for smallpox. Since there is also a danger of unimmunized infants transferring rubella to pregnant women, immunizing all infants against rubella decreases this risk, too.

Another precaution against rubella is a routine blood test administered during pregnancy or shortly after birth to see if a mother is immune or susceptible to the disease. If the mother is rubella-susceptible, her doctor will usually give her the rubella vaccine right after delivery. Approximately 85 percent of women in the United States are already immune to rubella.

Keep in mind that good science is usually good sense. It doesn't make sense that there would be a link between the rubella vaccine and autism if the vaccine were given at one year versus eighteen months. However, if your wife feels better giving your daughter the vaccine at eighteen months, there is certainly no risk in waiting.

☙

Chicken Pox Vaccine: Risks vs. Benefits

Q *My pediatrician says that it's not clear whether girls should get the chicken pox vaccine. He says immunity from* *the vaccine might wear off by the time a woman is of child-bearing age, and if she were to get chicken pox during pregnancy or while nursing, it could be serious. He says that it might be better if she got chicken pox as a child and developed natural immunities. Should I vaccinate my daughter?*

A Chicken pox (also called varicella) can cause more than just an itchy night or a spotted child. It often translates into a miserable week—or more—for the entire family: Children lose sleep and miss school; parents lose sleep and miss work. And when this highly contagious disease is spread to a sibling, the cycle continues.

Complications, though uncommon, can occur. Some children develop a bacterial infection, such as pneumonia or an ear infection, and may require hospitalization. When an adult gets chicken pox, the disease is usually more severe and often turns into pneumonia. If a pregnant woman catches chicken pox, there is a chance that her baby will develop complications. According to the American Academy of Pediatrics (AAP), each year about nine thousand people in the United States are hospitalized for chicken pox, and about ninety people die from the disease.

The varicella vaccine (VARIVAX) will protect children from these risks. However, statistics show that not enough parents are giving the shot to their kids. According to the Centers for Disease Control and Prevention, only 26 percent of children ages nineteen to thirty-five months have received the vaccine. The AAP recommends that a single dose of the vaccine be added to the list of routine immunizations for children between twelve and eighteen months of age who do not have a history of the disease. Older children who haven't been immunized should receive a single dose. Teens (thirteen years and over) and adults require two doses, spaced four to eight weeks apart. At this point, the vaccine seems to be 70 to 90 percent effective; if vaccinated children do get the chicken pox, the disease is much less severe.

The question of whether the vaccine's immunity will wear off, especially when women are of childbearing age, is one that has arisen with every new vaccine. Yet all vaccines seem to confer lifelong immunity. While it's too early to know whether this will be the case with the chicken pox vaccine, it has been used in millions of children throughout Japan, Korea, and Europe, and follow-up studies twelve years later show that it continues to provide protection. Even if immunity doesn't last, your daughter can receive a booster of the vaccine as a teenager or adult.

In our opinion, the chicken pox vaccine's benefits far outweigh the risks, which are minimal. After receiving the vaccine, about 5 percent of children get a mild case of chicken pox, which is usually limited to a mild fever and half a dozen spots. Some children experience swelling and tenderness at the injection site.

✍

Breastfeeding and Ear Infections

Q *My baby gets lots of ear infections. I often nurse him lying down, especially during nighttime feedings. I've read that fluids can enter the middle ear when a baby drinks from a bottle while lying down. Does this also apply to breastfeeding?*

A Yes. Any type of feeding—by bottle or breast—while lying down can contribute to ear infections.

When a baby lies horizontal, milk can travel up the throat from the eustachian tube and into the middle ear, setting up a culture medium that allows bacteria to grow in the eustachian tube or behind the eardrum. This happens much less frequently with breastfeeding babies, however. Breast milk contains natural antibodies, while formula can be more irritating to the middle-ear structures.

To reduce the possibility of ear infections, prop your baby up at least 30 degrees during feedings. The easiest way to do this is to place your arm under his head and shoulders while nursing.

✍

Heart Murmur

Q *At a recent well-baby checkup, we learned that our six-month-old girl has a heart murmur. She seems healthy otherwise (she weighs 15 pounds and is 25 inches long), but our doctor set up an ultrasound. Should we be worried?*

A Chances are you have nothing to worry about. A heart murmur is simply an extra noise in the heart sounds. Children's hearts beat faster than adults', and blood flowing quickly through the heart valves often causes an extra noise. Sometimes a fever or other condition can cause the heart to beat fast and blood to flow faster through the heart, which produces an innocent murmur. Approximately 40 percent of all infants have a normal, or innocent, murmur that usually disappears as the child grows. Some people retain a harmless murmur throughout their lives.

When a doctor listens to a child's heart with a stethoscope, it is often impossible to tell whether the murmur is normal or if there is a problem with the structure of the heart (such as a narrowed valve or an extra opening between chambers). So the next step is to order an ultrasound. This painless procedure—similar to the one you had during childbirth checkups—will detect whether or not your child's heart is structurally normal.

The term "heart murmur" tends to cause needless anxiety. In most cases the murmur is simply a variant of normal heart sounds. In my pediatrics practice, I always mention a heart murmur to parents as your doctor did if I hear one during routine checkups, and I explain what it means. That way, if the child is examined by another doctor who notices a murmur, the parents are familiar with the term.

Try not to worry about your baby's heart murmur. If the ultrasound is normal, it's not even necessary to mention it on a health or life insurance form. Chances are the extra sound will fade as your child grows.

Kidney Reflux

Q *What is kidney reflux, and why does it occur?*

A Normally urine is produced in the kidneys and travels down to the bladder through two tubes called ureters. When the bladder contracts to push urine out, muscular valves close at the junction of the urethra and bladder, preventing urine from traveling back up the ureters (refluxing) into the kidneys. Some children are born with inefficient valves, so when the bladder contracts, the urine is pushed back up into the kidneys. Constantly bombarding the kidneys with refluxed urine can lead to kidney infections and eventual kidney damage. This is why your doctor will manage this condition carefully.

If reflux is identified and managed correctly in the early years (before kidney damage occurs), a baby should grow up with a completely normal urinary tract. The first step is to identify the presence and severity of reflux. This is usually done initially by an ultrasound of the kidneys and bladder, often followed by an X-ray study of the bladder, ureters, and kidneys. Once the doctor has determined the staging of the reflux, he or she will outline a treatment plan. The treatment plan can range from doing frequent urine cultures to be sure no infection is present to taking long-term daily antibiotics to keep the urine sterile and prevent infection to yearly X rays. If the reflux worsens despite medical treatment, surgical re-implantation of the ureters may be necessary.

We cannot overemphasize the importance of early diagnosis and proper management of kidney reflux by a team consisting of you, a pediatric nephrologist (kidney specialist), and a pediatric urologist (urinary tract specialist).

☙

Constipation from Iron-Fortified Formula

Q *Can the iron in infant formula cause constipation? My ten-week-old baby is constipated, although I give him up to 4 ounces of water each day. We feed him Isomil (he became congested with a cow's-milk formula). If changing the formula doesn't help, what should I try next?*

A Opinion is divided on whether the iron in infant formula can cause constipation. Controlled studies performed by the late Dr. Frank Oski, Professor and Chairman of the Department of Pediatrics at Johns Hopkins Medical School, showed that iron-fortified formulas did not cause constipation any more than formulas without iron. But scientific research and mothers' firsthand observations sometimes clash. In our pediatrics practice, a mother occasionally tells us she's absolutely certain that iron causes constipation. You've observed the same with your baby.

While you may find that iron in infant formula makes your baby constipated, your baby still needs an iron-fortified formula. Low-iron formulas simply don't provide adequate amounts of iron, resulting in anemia (low hemoglobin) between the ages of six and twelve months.

Here are some ways to relieve your baby's constipation:

- Continue giving him an extra 4 to 8 ounces of water a day.
- Experiment with different types of formula until you find one that is more intestines friendly. Soy formula tends to be constipating, so you might try a predigested formula, such as Alimentum or Nutramigen. We recommend that you use these formulas as a last resort, since they are expensive and often unpalatable.
- Delay solid foods for several more months, since rice cereal and bananas (the usual starter foods) can be constipating.
- Feed your baby smaller amounts more frequently to aid digestion.
- Give your baby warm, daily baths while massaging his abdomen. This will help the stools move along through the intestines.
- If your baby strains during a bowel movement, insert half of an infant glycerin suppository into his rectum. These suppositories—available without prescription— resemble tiny rocket ships, and you can use them every couple of days for a few weeks without your baby becoming dependent on them.

Remember the four P's: prunes, pears, plums, and peaches. As he gets older—between seven and nine months—try adding prune or pear nectar and pureed prunes or pears to your baby's diet.

Use a low-iron formula for two more months if iron-fortified formula continues to constipate your baby. Then, once his intestines are more mature and his tolerance increases, you can switch back to an iron-fortified formula.

ℐ&

Homemade Baby Food

Q *My nine-month-old daughter has been eating stage-two commercial baby foods since she was four months old. Lately I've been trying to make her foods—beef, carrots and brown rice, or noodles and chicken—which are pureed but not as smoothly as in the jar. My daughter just leaves the food on her tongue or gags and doesn't seem to be able to swallow it. Do you think the smooth baby food has spoiled her? Shouldn't she be able to eat pieces of food by now? I'm afraid to keep trying as I don't want her to choke on anything she can't handle.*

A You are wise to take the time and energy to prepare your own baby food. It is more nutritious for your baby than commercially packaged foods. At nine months she is ready for less smoothly pureed foods, so don't give up.

Introducing solid foods to your baby exposes her to a variety of foods (in addition to breast milk and formula) and shapes her developing tastes. In fact, the foods that babies begin with become their norm, shaping their expectations of how food is supposed to taste. If your baby spends the first year eating primarily jarred or canned foods, she learns that this is what food is supposed to taste like. If, however, she eats primarily freshly prepared foods, she learns that the taste of fresh foods is the norm. Shaping your daughter's tastes early on for fresh foods over commercial ones can help her establish a lifelong preference for more nutritious eating patterns.

In addition to meeting nutritional needs, progressing to solid foods is also a developmental feat. If your baby prefers eating solids with her fingers rather than being spoon-fed, let her do so. It will help her develop her fine-motor skills, and a bit of a mess is part of the feeding game. If she completely shuns lumpy foods, stick with the smoother ones. When preparing homemade baby foods, experiment with consistency until you find the one that will get the most food down with the least amount of protest. Choose nutritious foods and present them creatively. For example, pureed avocados are an excellent source of nutrition at this age.

⟋⟍

Hip Dislocation

Q *My six-month-old baby girl was diagnosed with hip dislocation. Is this a serious condition?*

A Hip dislocation occurs when the socket of the pelvic bone is somewhat flattened instead of curved, allowing the "ball" of the leg bone to flip out or dislocate. The condition, which could affect your child's gait, is one of the most important things a pediatrician looks for during well-baby exams during the first six months, because the earlier hip dislocation is detected and treated, the better the outcome. If the pediatrician suspects hip dislocation, he or she will order an X ray or ultrasound to confirm the diagnosis.

The course of treatment depends on the severity of the dislocation, but in most cases the doctor will seek to stabilize the joint, keeping the legs apart and allowing the pelvic socket to grow around the ball of the leg bone.

If the hip joint is possibly dislocatable, your child will wear a harness that looks like a heavily padded diaper with suspenders. If the condition is more severe, she'll wear a rigid brace—something akin to a fiberglass diaper—for three to six months and will need follow-up exams and X rays. If you begin the treatment early, your baby will develop normal hips and walk normally.

Green Stools

Q *I've been feeding my two-month-old baby Carnation Good Start formula with iron, and her stools have turned dark green. Should I switch to formula without iron?*

A Don't worry about the change in the color of your baby's bowel movements or feel you have to change her formula. The iron in formulas normally turns babies' stools green. As long as she is thriving on the formula and does not have an irritating diaper rash, this is the right formula for her. We don't suggest that you give your baby a formula without iron. Babies need extra iron for healthy blood.

♋

Normal Soft Spots

Q *My six-week-old baby's soft spot goes straight across when I run my fingers over it. I thought all babies' soft spots should be concave. Should I be worried?*

A If your baby's soft spot is straight across, you don't have to worry. When you rub your fingers across the front of her head, her soft spot should feel flat. You need to worry only if the soft spot bulges outward like an egg. In that case, it will feel like a little hump when you run your fingers across it.

Be happy! It sounds like you have a healthy baby.

♋

Treating Infant Gassiness

Q *Our five-week-old baby has crying spells that last for up to an hour. During the spells, she passes gas. We recently switched from breastfeeding to bottlefeeding. The doctor says it takes a few weeks to adjust and that our baby's body is getting used to the formula. Is this correct?*

A The fact that your baby's upset began when you switched from breast milk to formula is a sign that she is allergic to the formula. Rather than continue with the same formula and run the risk of prolonged intestinal colic, we suggest that you experiment with various types of formulas and methods of feeding.

Formula contains protein and lactose, which can cause abdominal upset. So begin with formulas that vary these nutritional elements. To determine if your baby is lactose-intolerant, try a lactose-free formula for a week. If the gassiness persists, she may be allergic to cow's-milk protein. If that is the case, switch to a soy-based formula (such as Isomil or Enfamil ProSobee) for a week. If she is still gassy, try Alimentum or Pregestimil. Both are lactose-free and contain predigested cow's-milk protein, which makes them hypoallergenic. Smaller, more frequent feedings may also help your baby get used to digesting formula.

As your baby's intestines mature, the gassy stage will pass. In the meantime, though, here are ways to relieve her discomfort:

- *The gas pump.* Lay your baby on her back on your lap with her head resting on your knees and her legs pointing toward you. Pump her legs in a bicycling motion.
- *The colic curl.* Slide your baby's back down your chest and encircle your arms under her bottom. Curl baby up, facing forward, with her head and back resting against your chest. Or try reversing the position, holding your baby facing you with her feet against your chest. In this

position, you can maintain eye contact and play facial gesture games with your baby.

- *The tummy tuck.* Place a rolled-up cloth diaper or a warm (not hot) water bottle wrapped in a cloth diaper under your baby's tummy during gas pain. To further relax a tense tummy, lay baby stomach-down on a cushion with her legs dangling over the edge, and rub her back.

- *Tummy touches.* Place the palm of your hand over your baby's navel and let your finger and thumb encircle her abdomen. Let her lean her tense abdomen against your warm hand while she sits on your lap, feet facing you. Practice the "I Love U touch with your baby. Picture an upside-down *U* on your baby's abdomen. Rub some warm massage oil on your hands and knead baby's tense abdomen with your flattened fingers in a circular motion. Start with a downward stroke for the *I* on baby's left side, then massage along the upside-down *L* along the top of your baby's abdomen. Finally, massage along the upside-down *U*, stroking upward along the right, across, and down the left side.

⌇

Flushing Baby's Stuffed-Up Nose

Q *My nine-month-old son has a cold, and my wife and I have tried to flush his nose with saline nasal spray. But we find it difficult to administer the spray. Do you have any suggestions that could make this procedure easier?*

A Babies naturally resist any intrusion into their nasal passages, but it's important that your baby get used to the "hosing the nose" procedure. This is one of the most effective measures to keep a simple cold from progressing into a sinus or ear infection.

Instead of laying your baby on his back while flushing his nose—a position he'll find threatening and is likely to protest—sit him upright on your lap while flushing his nose. Gently squirt the saline nasal spray upward into his nasal passages and suction with a nasal aspirator.

If your baby absolutely hates the nose flushing, "steam clean" his nasal passages by holding him while you take a warm shower.

$\mathscr{L}$

Tracking Motor Development

Q *My twelve-month-old son seems normal in every way except that he doesn't pull himself up to a sitting or standing position. He can roll from front to back and back to front but seems content to sit or lie on his stomach. When he tries to crawl, he struggles and ends up pushing himself backward. Our pediatrician tells us his development is progressing, but we are sick with worry. He is a very docile child. What could be the problem?*

A Your doctor will evaluate your baby's motor development at each well-baby checkup. And as long as your pediatrician isn't worried, you needn't worry either. If an underlying developmental abnormality exists, it usually affects all forms of development—motor, social, and language development. As long as your child shows progressive motor development by doing more each month, there is no cause for alarm. In fact, there is a wide range of what is considered normal in motor development milestones. For example, the crab crawl (moving backward or sideways) that you describe is a normal development quirk that appears in some infants between nine and twelve months.

Good development means that each month your child will get more and more of his body off the ground. The important thing is that you see a gradual, steady progression from crawling to standing to walking. Here are some general milestones to look for in the coming months:

- 13 months: Standing supported
- 14 months: Letting go with one hand
- 15 months: Cruising around furniture while holding on
- 15 to 18 months: Walking

A final word about worry: Love for your child will naturally bring out your anxiety. Your doctor's job is to reassure you, whether or not you have anything to worry about. It's important that you not convey your anxiety to your child. If your child constantly reads worry on your face rather than joy, this certainly will not contribute to his overall development. Each child develops at his own pace. Do the best you can to convey messages of joy to your child and leave the worrying to your doctor.

Fifth Disease

Q   *I think my daughter has fifth disease. How can I be sure? How contagious is this disease, and should I be worried? I am pregnant.*

A   Fifth disease (so named because it was the fifth virus discovered to cause fever and rash) is a common childhood viral illness that is contagious but seldom harmful to children or adults. The disease is diagnosed from the appearance of a red rash on the face that looks like slapped cheeks. A lacy red rash may also appear on the legs and trunk of the body. Adults with this illness may have sore joints. Fifth disease is contagious for up to a week before the facial rash appears.

Although the virus is usually harmless to children, there are special concerns if you are pregnant. The good news is that most adults are already immune to the fifth disease virus, so the virus is unlikely to be transmitted to your preborn baby during pregnancy. If you are not already immune, the main concern is a slight increase (1 to 2 percent) in the risk of miscarriage if you are exposed during the first trimester of your pregnancy. If you are exposed to fifth disease during the last trimester of pregnancy, the virus could break down some of the baby's red blood cells, causing anemia. However, the anemia is unlikely to be severe enough to harm the baby.

If you are worried about the effects of your exposure on your preborn baby, ask your doctor to do a blood test to see if you are immune to fifth disease. If you are, there is no need to worry. Even if you are not immune, you may not have been infected with the virus despite close exposure to your child. Your doctor can do a second blood test to show if you have been recently infected with the fifth disease virus. If the test results are negative, you have nothing to worry about. If you were infected with fifth disease, your baby has only a very slight risk of being harmed.

ᘓ

Ear Infections

Q *What is the best treatment for ear infections? I keep hearing about new studies that claim less is best when it comes to antibiotics.*

A   It is natural to be confused with all the conflicting advice on how to treat ear infections. It's true that many ear infections go away without antibiotics; those caused by a virus are healed by the body's own natural defenses. The problem is that when a child has a sore red ear, it is hard to tell whether the infection is viral or bacterial. If the infection is bacterial and it is not treated with an antibiotic, the child's eardrum could rupture. In this case, the child often winds up needing a stronger antibiotic for a longer time, when a seven-day course of a milder antibiotic would have cleared up the infection in the first place.

After nearly thirty years in pediatrics, I have come to the conclusion that it's better to be aggressive in treating ear infections. However, antibiotics, while helpful, kill only the germs in the middle ear.

Here are some natural remedies to try before or in addition to antibiotics:

- Keep your child's nose clean with saltwater nasal spray and a suction bulb. This will lessen the frequency and severity of ear infections.
- Minimize your child's exposure to allergens, including cigarette smoke, animal dander, and dust. Exposure to allergens causes fluid in the middle ear, which creates an environment conducive to bacteria. Cigarette smoke is one of the most commonly overlooked causes of ear infections. Dust often permeates a youngster's fuzzy toy–filled bedroom.
- Monitor your child's exposure to contagious children. Be sure your day-care center has strict rules about keeping contagious children at home.
- Breastfeed for as long as possible. The incidence of ear infections in breastfed babies is much lower than in formula-fed infants.
- Feed your baby in an upright position. This will keep milk and other fluids from going into the middle ear (which can happen when babies drink lying down).

Finally, if your child gets frequent ear infections, bear in mind that hearing loss from undertreated ear infections is more debilitating than the minimal problems associated with long-term antibiotic use.

℘

Ear Infections and
Speech Development

Q *After months of recurrent ear infections, my twenty-month-old son recently had tubes put in his ears. We thought that he would start talking once he got the tubes, but he hasn't. We believe he can hear us because he responds to commands, such as, "Please shut the door." What should we do?*

A Recurrent ear infections can cause fluid to build up behind the eardrum. Then, when sound waves enter the ear, the fluid dampens the eardrum's vibration, diminishing a child's ability to hear. Once the fluid drains, which can happen either on its own or through the use of antibiotics or tubes, normal hearing quickly returns. Tubes ensure continued drainage of the fluid.

The chronic presence of fluid in the ear may have delayed your son's speech development by a few months, but he should catch up soon. Each toddler develops speech at a different rate. One might show a steady, word-a-day increase in vocabulary, while another will jabber in bursts of new words. And many toddlers, especially boys, don't say much until around their second birthday, as if they are storing words for their two-year opening speech.

In normal speech development, many twenty-month-old toddlers are at the "understands everything, says little" stage. They can communicate; they just don't talk. Instead, they use body language to express themselves. How many words your son uses is not as important as how well he communicates.

To be sure your son is developing on track, do your own at-home hearing check. Pay attention to your son when you give him simple commands, such as, "Shut the door" or "Go get the ball." Does he follow your requests only if he watches your face intently while you speak? If so, he may be lipreading and should have his hearing checked. If not, then his hearing is probably normal. If your son passes this test, chart his speech progress over the next four months by recording his words and phrases. If he adds a few words of increasing complexity each month, his speech is developing normally. On the other hand, if he isn't expanding his vocabulary or understanding simple requests, we recommend he undergo hearing testing and begin speech therapy.

✑

Drool Rash and Other Teething Trials

Q *My seven-month-old son had his first two bottom teeth pop through at six months. He has a terrible drool rash, and I think the top teeth are on the way. How soon should I expect the top teeth? Other than Tylenol and top-ical rubs, what else can I do to help my child during this difficult time? Finally, what can I do for the teething facial rash?*

A It sounds like your baby is already experiencing discomfort from his erupting top teeth. Expect them to pop through within the next month. Acetaminophen (Tylenol) can ease his teething pain. You can also let your baby gnaw on something cold—an ice cube inside a baby sock, a cold washcloth, or a cold rubber teething ring, for example.

Sensitive skin and excessive saliva are an uncomfortable mix, especially when your baby's cheeks are rubbing against a drool-soaked bed sheet. Rather than letting your baby sleep cheek to sheet, place him to sleep on his back. Or put a drool-absorbing cotton diaper under baby's chin while he sleeps. When saliva drool collects in the fat folds of that adorable little double chin, gently pat the excess drool off his skin with lukewarm water. Then apply an emollient, such as Soothe and Heal with Lansinoh, to the drool-sensitive areas as a barrier ointment. In addition to causing a rash, excess saliva dripping down the back of your baby's throat can give him an irritating but harmless cough.

As a final note, expect loose stools and a mild diaper rash during teething time. If your baby's bottom becomes irritated, apply the same emollient mentioned above.

Diarrhea

Q *Our five-month-old daughter has had diarrhea for more than ten days. I've been breastfeeding her, but during the last few weeks we have given her some bottled milk because my milk supply has dropped. Our baby has no fever or any other symptoms of illness, but her stool is still green in color. Could her diarrhea be caused by something I am eating?*

A Your baby's diarrhea is most likely due to an intestinal infection. As long as she does not have a fever, abdominal pain, or increasing weight loss, there is no need to worry.

Two types of germs cause diarrhea in infants: viruses and bacteria. Viral infections are usually a nuisance type of diarrhea in an otherwise well baby, and they heal themselves without treatment. Bacterial infections are usually associated with fever, abdominal pain, and increasing weight loss; your child may need an antibiotic. Let the old saying "no weight loss, no problem" be your guide. If your baby isn't losing weight, and if she isn't particularly bothered by the diarrhea, it will probably go away without treatment.

Keep in mind, however, that the intestines are slow to heal; it could take six to eight weeks for your baby's bowel movements to return to their normal consistency. Breast milk helps the intestines heal and is best tolerated by an irritated intestinal lining. Cow's milk, on the other hand, may aggravate the diarrhea. Try nursing your baby more often to increase your milk supply. If she needs a supplement, a soy-based formula would be more intestines friendly.

Your main goal in treating diarrhea is to prevent your baby from getting dehydrated, and weight loss is one sign of dehydration. To provide additional fluids, feed her an oral rehydration solution, such as Pedialyte, or 2 ounces of diluted white grape juice several times a day. Unlike other fruit juices, which may worsen diarrhea, white grape juice contains the type of sugar that makes it intestines friendly.

☙

Crib Head Banging

Q *My one-year-old son rocks in his crib. When he does this, he slams his head into the end of the crib with such force that he has given himself bruises (he can move his crib across a hardwood floor). Apparently I did the same thing when I was a baby, but I am concerned about this behavior. Any comments?*

A Many infants bang their heads in their cribs without harming themselves. But it's wise to take any disturbing behavior as a signal to intervene before it gets worse. Head banging can be a sign that a child needs to be gentled, mellowed, and organized. The best way to organize a baby is to wear him around the house several hours a day in a baby sling. This provides vestibular stimulation: the rhythm of your walk and the closeness to your body relax an infant and make him less prone to such self-destructive behaviors as head banging.

Head banging in a crib may also be a sign that your little one feels confined and can't relax "behind bars." Try a co-sleeper, a criblike infant bed that attaches to the side of your bed and puts baby within arm's reach of Mom, close enough for touching and nursing. At the same time, baby has his own sleeping space. We recommend the

Arm's Reach Co-Sleeper. Visit www.armsreach.com to find a retailer near you. Use caution if you try to make your own co-sleeper by removing a side rail from your baby's crib and placing the crib adjacent to your bed. The crib can move away from the bed, leaving a gap in which baby can get trapped or into which he can fall.

✑

Cooling a Burning Bottom

Q *My daughter has diarrhea and a severe rash on her bottom. Our pediatrician suggested applying Maalox or Mylanta to her rear end for the acid burn. He said it would neutralize the acid that comes out in her diarrhea and irritates her skin. Is this okay to do, or is my doctor weird?*

A Let's first consider where your baby's rash comes from. Start with ultrasensitive skin, add the chemicals in urine and stools, cover the area with a big "bandage," and rub it all together. Presto! You have diaper rash. If you keep this mixture together long enough, bacteria and fungi will begin to grow into the weakened skin, increasing the rash. Then, when the moist fat folds rub together, the rash spreads to the creases of the groin.

What enters your baby's mouth further affects the skin on her rear end. Antibiotics, change of diet, and excess saliva during teething may all lead to diarrhea, which causes the acid burn on your baby's bottom. Since I have no experience using Maalox or Mylanta on babies' bottoms, let me suggest a more conventional treatment:

- Use ultra-absorbent diapers to keep your baby's skin as dry as possible.
- Rinse baby's bottom after every diaper change. Sensitive skin does best with plain water, although some bottoms need a mild soap. Sore bottoms may react to the chemicals in disposable baby wipes—especially those containing alcohol.
- Dip baby's bottom in a baking soda bath (add ¼ cup of baking soda to her bath water) to neutralize the acid.
- Blot the skin dry with a soft towel and avoid excessive rubbing or scrubbing with a strong soap on irritated skin. One of our babies had such sensitive skin that even towel blotting reddened it. Instead, we used a hair dryer (held 12 inches away on the lowest setting) to blow-dry her bottom.
- Keep bottoms up. Expose baby's bottom to the air while she is sleeping and occasionally to a ten-minute ray of sunlight through a closed window.
- Apply a lubricant, such as Soothe and Heal with Lansinoh, as a barrier cream.

Diaper rash is an unfortunate fact of life for bottom-covered babies. But like all the other nuisance stages of infancy, it too will pass.

♉

Treating Bowel Discomfort

Q *My four-month-old baby makes a terrible gasping sound after each bowel movement. The sound gets worse if we lay her on her back immediately after she is done. She is on medication to relieve her cramping and bowel spasms.*

A The gasping sounds your baby is making are probably the result of intestinal pain. One cause of this could be a milk or formula allergy. If you are breastfeeding, your infant may be intolerant of something in your diet—dairy products, corn, nuts, or caffeine-containing foods, such as colas, tea, and coffee. If you are formula feeding, try a less allergenic preparation. Begin with soy formulas and progress to the least allergenic formulas (Alimentum, Nutramigen, and Pregestimil).

When your baby feels gassy and bloated, put her in a warm bath and massage her abdomen, or lay her on the floor and pump her legs in a bicycling motion. If she strains to have a bowel movement, a tiny bullet-size infant glycerin suppository (available over the counter) may help. Finally, increasing the amount of water she drinks will loosen the stools and make it easier for her to pass them.

Your baby may have gastroesophageal reflux, discussed on page 13. With GER, stomach acids are regurgitated into the esophagus after eating, causing a heartburnlike pain. The strain of having a bowel movement could trigger reflux, causing your baby to gasp in

pain. Keep her upright (at at least a 45-degree angle) for
half an hour after each feeding, and place her on her
tummy after feeding when she is awake (reflux is often
worsened when baby lies on her back). Babies usually outgrow reflux by eight months, when they are able to sit up
after feeding.

✍

Colic Means My Baby Is Hurting

Q *My three-month-old baby girl was born ten weeks
early. I stopped breastfeeding at seven weeks and have
been giving her formula. She began eating a lot (6 to 9
ounces at a feeding) and became constipated. My pediatrician suggested that I stop feeding her so much, but now
my baby has colic. Although she has no temperature, she
is sleeping more than usual. Today she woke up with a
hoarse cry. Is this normal for colicky babies because they
scream so much?*

A Here is a trade secret we have learned from almost
thirty years practicing pediatrics: Colic is a five-letter
word that means "the doctor doesn't know." In our view, it
is too easy to tag a baby as colicky and quickly dismiss the
problem. We prefer the phrase "hurting baby" to "colicky
baby."

Colic can stem from a variety of causes. Your baby may
hurt because she is allergic to the formula. In fact, anytime
you see a change in behavior or bowel habits following a

change in feeding, it's reasonable to suspect that the food and the intestines don't agree with one another. Gastroesophageal reflux (GER), as discussed on page 13, is another hidden cause of colicky behavior.

To make feeding less hurtful and more pleasant for your baby, try changing formulas. Milk-based formulas are most likely the cause of her discomfort because of an allergy to the protein in milk. Try switching to a soy-based formula. But before making the switch, take note of your baby's usual symptoms so that you can objectively record any changes. If you notice no improvement after a week on soy formula, try a hypoallergenic formula, such as Alimentum, Nutramigen, or Pregestimil. In these protein-hydrolysate formulas, the potentially allergenic proteins have been predigested, so they're easier on baby's digestive system. Also, try smaller, more frequent feedings. Some babies, while not allergic to formula itself, simply can't digest too much at one feeding. But overfeeding is probably not the cause of your baby's constipation. It is more likely to cause diarrhea than constipation. Constipation does, however, sometimes mimic colic, resulting in a misdiagnosis. Give your baby an extra 8 ounces of water each day and experiment with formulas that are less constipating. If she strains to have a bowel movement, insert half of an infant glycerin suppository (available over the counter) into her rectum to make it easier for her to move her bowels.

The fact that your baby seems to be sleeping more than usual makes us doubt that a formula allergy or GER is at the root of her discomfort. Babies with intestinal upset usually sleep less and wake up frequently with painful cries. Crying accompanied by more sleeping suggests an emotional reason for your baby's discomfort rather than a dietary or medical one—though babies can hurt so much for medical reasons that they sleep more, simply out of exhaustion from crying. Has there been a recent change in caregivers, sleeping arrangements, or the family's lifestyle? If you have recently returned to work, try carrying her in a sling as much as you can on your days off to see if this settles her crying.

Your baby's excessive crying may be the cause of her hoarseness. But it is unusual even for colicky babies to be hoarse. The fact that your little one is crying herself hoarse is all the more reason to get to the bottom of why she is hurting. Keep working to identify any dietary or caregiver changes until you are able to ease your baby's discomfort. Colicky behavior that continues beyond six months strongly suggests an underlying medical cause, but the good news is that even unexplained colic usually passes by six months.

☙

Combating Constipation

Q *My sixteen-month-old son has trouble moving his bowels, even though we're giving him a daily doctor-recommended dose of Senokot Children's Syrup. We're also trying to alter his diet to include more fiber and vegetables. Still, he's having trouble passing the stools. He cries, screams, draws his legs into his chest, and even throws up from pushing so hard. It has been this way for nine months. Is it normal for this problem to persist for so long? What else can we do? And are we missing something medically?*

A Constipation can be a painful cycle. Your baby's bowel movements become hard and painful, usually because of a dietary change. This causes him to hold them in, which makes them harder and more difficult to pass. Over time the bowel muscle weakens, and that further aggravates the problem. It takes about six weeks of stool softening for the bowel muscle to regain its strength.

Try to increase the amount of fluid in his diet, making sure that he gets at least 32 ounces a day. In addition to milk, formula, and water, try prune, pear, or apricot nectar. Nectar has more pulp and therefore more fiber than strained juice.

Add fiber-rich foods to your baby's diet, such as whole-grain breads, graham crackers, bran cereals, and high-fiber vegetables, like broccoli, peas, and kidney beans. Make a puree of high-fiber fruits to spread on whole-grain bread. Use the "four P's"—prunes, pears, plums, and peaches—to make the puree.

You might also make him a daily smoothie of fresh fruits. Strawberries, blueberries, and papaya are excellent fiber sources, and papaya is especially intestines friendly. Add 2 teaspoons of flax oil, a nutritious supplement (available at your health-food store) that contributes to stool softening.

Watch for his "about to go" signals of squatting and straining. You may have to ease the passage of hard stools by using a daily glycerin suppository for a few days. Once the stools are softer, you will find that he will not refuse to pass them.

Cephalohematoma

Q *When our son was born we noticed he had a lump on the back of his head. The doctor told us this was normal, but we are getting worried. He is seven weeks old now, and we can still feel the lump.*

A The lump you are feeling is called a cephalo-hematoma, which is caused by tiny blood vessels beneath the scalp breaking during delivery. This "goose egg" type of lump could take several months to disappear and may feel increasingly hard as the underlying blood calcifies. These lumps are harmless and happen in most babies during passage through the birth canal.

Because the lump is in the scalp and not actually in the brain, the bleeding will not bother your baby. Again, don't be alarmed if you still feel a slight lump a year later. If this were anything more than normal newborn scalp bleeding, your doctor would have informed you.

Choking Spells

Q *My three-month-old baby was born prematurely at thirty weeks. A month ago he was diagnosed with reflux.*

*The doctor put him on Tagamet and Bethanecol, and I
thicken his formula with rice cereal. The choking spells
are not as frequent as they were before, but some are quite
severe (during one episode, I thought I would have to do
CPR, but he finally breathed on his own). Our pediatrician
says our baby just has to outgrow these spells, but my husband and I find them very scary.*

A Gastroesophageal reflux (GER) occurs in varying
degrees in as many as a third of babies under six months
of age. It is a common hidden cause of colic and choking
episodes. Normally the muscular ring at the junction of the
esophagus and stomach acts as a one-way valve. When the
stomach contracts, the ring tightens and keeps the stomach
contents from backing up (refluxing) into the esophagus.
In some infants this ring is weak, and reflux occurs.

Your infant is on the right medications to cut down on
stomach acid and increase the rate of stomach emptying. In
addition to the treatment you are now giving him,
remember that gravity is a regurgitator's best friend.

Follow the tips on pages 13–14 to reduce reflux and the
subsequent pain and spitting up. Also experiment with different formulas to see which stays down the best. And try
different nipples until you find one that minimizes the
amount of air he swallows.

Your baby is near the peak age for severe reflux (usually around four months). To help your doctor adjust the
type and dosage of his medications, keep a record to monitor signs that the reflux is getting better or worse. Note
any colic, spitting up, choking, or stop-breathing episodes.
As a valuable part of the medical partnership, it is important for you to be a keen observer and accurate reporter.

The good news is that in most infants, reflux begins to
subside at around eight months, when the muscular ring

matures and baby spends more of the day in an upright position.

⟡

Caffeine During Pregnancy and SIDS

Q *Is it true that drinking coffee during pregnancy increases the risk of SIDS? I'm in my first trimester, and I still enjoy a daily cup of coffee, but I don't want to harm my unborn baby. Should I give up caffeine?*

A Because SIDS is linked to a defect in the automatic control of breathing during sleep, it makes sense that any chemical that can interfere with the development of the respiratory control system in utero could increase the risk of SIDS.

Caffeine has always been on the suspicious list of drugs that could interfere with fetal development. In fact, for the past decade pregnant women have been advised to limit their intake of caffeine to reduce the risk of miscarriage and low birth weight.

A study published recently in the *Archives of Disease in Childhood* suggests that drinking four or more cups of coffee a day throughout pregnancy nearly doubles the risk of SIDS. Of course, this is a statistical link, and more research needs to be done to prove a connection.

However, since most pregnant women develop a natural aversion to caffeine, it's highly unusual for a pregnant woman to drink four cups of coffee on a daily basis. I suspect that the mothers in the caffeine-linked study had other unhealthy habits that could have increased their risk of losing a baby to SIDS.

While results of the caffeine study are preliminary and need to be replicated, three factors have been recognized as crucial to lowering the risk of SIDS.

1. Avoid smoking, pre- and postnatally.
2. Put your baby to sleep on her back.
3. Breastfeed.

Over the past five years, SIDS rates throughout the world have fallen. In some countries the incidence of SIDS has dropped by 50 percent. The current SIDS rate in the United States is 0.8 per thousand infants. Some doctors attribute this decline to the fact that more parents are putting their infants to sleep on their backs instead of on their sides or stomachs.

Good Health for Bottlefed Babies

Q *For medical reasons I will not be able to breastfeed my baby. What extra precautions can I take to ensure my baby's health and meet her nutritional needs?*

A Your doctor can help you choose the right formula to meet your baby's nutritional needs. But there are many other things you can do to promote your baby's physical and nutritional health.

- *Eat well during pregnancy.* Nurturing your baby begins in the womb. Take good nutritional care of yourself during your pregnancy to give your preborn baby a healthy start. You will find useful information about a complete program of nutrition and exercise in *The Pregnancy Book* (Little, Brown, 1997).
- *Stay in touch.* Research shows that touching and interacting with a baby stimulates her physical, emotional, and intellectual health. Hold your infant as much as you can during the first year, providing lots of eye-to-eye and skin-to-skin contact. This physical closeness will enhance your connection with your little one and help your baby get smart from the start.
- *Make feedings special.* Two aspects of the breastfeeding relationship contribute to an infant's sense of well-being: the nutrients in the milk itself; and the increased holding that breastfed babies get. As well as delivering nutrition, feeding is a social interaction. When bottle-feeding, cuddle your baby as much as you would if you were nursing.
- *Wear your baby in a baby sling as much as possible.* In addition to providing physical contact, the motion of being carried will enhance your little one's growth by providing the calming effects of movement.
- *Share sleep.* Sleeping with your baby provides the security of nighttime touch and enhances emotional development. This is especially important for parents who work outside the home. High-touch nighttime parenting will

allow you to reconnect with your baby at night and make up for missed touch time during the day.

Above all, respond to baby's cues in a nurturing way. Ignore any advice to let your baby cry it out. The key word for infant development is "responsiveness." Years ago at an annual meeting of the American Academy of Pediatrics, Dr. Michael Lewis, Professor of Pediatrics at Rutgers University, reported that after reviewing all the scientific studies on what makes babies smarter and healthier, he found the most important factor to be the caregivers' responsiveness to the baby's cues.

The parenting style you choose is crucial to your infant's development, and making yourself available and responding to baby's cues in a nurturing way are vitally important to giving your baby the healthiest start possible.

⟋⟋⟍

Bellybutton Basics

Q How soon after the umbilical cord stump falls off can I give my baby a bath?

A If the site where the cord was attached is completely dry and there is no redness around the edges (usually by two weeks), it is safe to immerse your baby in a bath. The key is to avoid infection in the cord area. If there is pus draining at the base of the cord, it is unwise to immerse baby in a bath for fear of contaminating the water and spreading the infection. In this case, you should sponge-bathe baby until the cord falls off and the stump is healed.

ℐↄ

Excessive Vomiting

Q *My four-month-old daughter vomits immediately after feeding and for several hours afterward. She does this with every type of formula and when breastfed. I know it's normal for babies to spit up small amounts occasionally, but she vomits at least an ounce of every feeding. We're sure she isn't eating too much. She weighed 10 pounds 3 ounces at birth and now weighs 14 pounds 6 ounces. She has a hearty appetite and takes half a dozen 6- to 7-ounce bottles a day, with occasional solid food. Two doctors have told us that our baby's vomiting is normal, but we are very concerned.*

A Your gut feeling is that there is something wrong with your baby's digestion, and you're probably right. Some degree of spitting up is normal in most babies. But normal spitting up gradually decreases in frequency and volume as a baby grows.

It sounds like your baby suffers from gastroesophageal reflux (GER), explained on page 13. Although your baby is putting on weight, the weight gain may not be optimal. Your baby could be growing but not thriving. It's important to ask your pediatrician to evaluate your child for

GER. It would also be wise for your infant to have an upper GI series. In this test, your daughter swallows barium, and an X ray traces the barium as it travels through the stomach and into the intestines. The results will indicate whether there is a partial obstruction at the outlet of the stomach that could be aggravating the reflux, causing her to spit up more. If there is no obstruction, you can look forward to life without spit-up. Most infants outgrow GER by eight months of age. Check out the suggestions on pages 13–14 to ease your baby's intestinal discomfort.

❧

Cold-Induced Asthma

Q *My three-year-old daughter has cold-induced asthma. Our doctor recommended albuterol and Intal every four hours for her cough. But my friend's pediatrician has her alternate these medications with an albuterol-and-saline solution for her asthmatic child. Which treatment is better for asthma flare-ups?*

A Since asthma varies from child to child, it is best to follow your own doctor's advice. Albuterol, a bronchodilator, is used to treat asthma when it starts or to prevent a cold or allergen from triggering an asthma attack. Intal (chromolyn sodium) is a preventive medicine that makes the respiratory tract less reactive to allergens. In a child with chronic asthma, Intal is normally used for daily maintenance (two to four times daily) with albuterol added during flare-ups. If your child has frequent asthma attacks during the cold season, ask your doctor about keeping her on daily Intal inhalations and using albuterol less frequently (and only as soon as the asthma begins).

⚘

Allergic Reaction to Strawberries

Q *My ten-month-old son recently reacted with vomiting and hives after eating a commercial baby food containing strawberries. Does this mean he'll have a more serious reaction to fresh strawberries? Should I be concerned about other fruits as well?*

A Strawberries contain a common food allergen that is best avoided by babies under the age of one year. The good news, however, is that infants outgrow most of their food allergies by two years of age.

Subsequent ingestion of strawberries could result in a more severe allergic reaction, so avoid feeding your son strawberries for at least six months and be sure to mention his strawberry allergy to substitute caregivers or anyone who might have occasion to feed your baby.

As a precaution, stay away from citrus fruits for a few months. Your baby doesn't need strawberries or citrus fruits at this age. He can get all the necessary nutrients from a balanced diet of breast milk or formula, grains, and vegetables, as well as less allergenic fruits (pears, applesauce, papayas, and bananas).

As your baby's intestines grow, the allergens are less likely to be absorbed through the intestines into the bloodstream. But just to be on the safe side, when you give him strawberries again (at around two years of age), do it gradually. Begin with half a strawberry once a day for a few days and see what happens.

≈

Making Sure Baby Gets Enough Breast Milk

Q *I recently watched an episode of a popular medical drama on television in which a baby died of "insufficient milk syndrome." I'm planning to breastfeed, and I know many mothers nurse without a problem. But what signs should I look for to make sure that this isn't a problem for me?*

A We also watched that episode. The moral of that story was watch your baby carefully and know when to seek medical help before you wind up with an emergency.

Typically a breastfed newborn gains 4 to 8 ounces a week during the first four months. In the first weeks, however, such small gains are not easy to see, especially if you are a first-time mother. This is why, when you leave the hospital, your doctor will schedule an office visit for a weight check, as well as to tell you what warning signs to watch for. After your baby is a month or two old, you probably won't need to monitor her so closely. You will come to recognize the signs that she is getting her fill. You will know that she is well nourished by her firm, smooth skin and by the fact that she gradually looks and feels heavier.

Insufficient milk syndrome has two causes: inadequate fluid volume, which causes dehydration, and inadequate calories, which can cause hunger and weight loss. Babies who are dehydrated have dry eyes and a dry mouth and dry, wrinkled skin, and they act sick (fussy and irritable) or lethargic and very sleepy. Sometimes babies can get plenty of milk but not enough calories, although they don't act sick. In our office we sometimes see babies who are not getting enough breast milk. They are usually not dehydrated as we can see by their activity, their wet diapers, and their wet mouth and eyes, but they are not gaining weight and are starting to look scrawny.

To better understand insufficient milk syndrome, let's take a quick look at breast milk. It is composed of two parts: the nutrient-rich foremilk, which pools at the front of your breasts and which your baby ingests first during a nursing, and the calorie-rich hindmilk, which your infant gets when he has finished the foremilk. The hindmilk comprises most of the calories in your breasts and fills the stomach. Babies often drop contentedly off to sleep after they have had their fill.

These steps will help you make sure that your newborn is getting enough of what she needs from your milk:

- *Monitor her wet diapers.* Remember, output equals input. If your baby is wetting enough diapers, she is getting enough milk and is safe from dehydration. When your milk comes in—after the first three or four days of nursing—your baby should wet six to eight cloth diapers every day (or four to six disposable ones, which hold more). If she does, you don't have to worry about dehydration.

- *Check her stools.* This will give you a clue as to whether or not your newborn is getting enough of the high-calorie hindmilk. In the first couple of weeks, she should have at least two bowel movements a day. In the first few days, her stools should go from sticky black to green to brown. Toward the end of the first week, as soon as your rich, creamy hindmilk comes in, the stools will become more yellow. If her stools have the color and consistency of yellow, seedy mustard, if she seems content, if her mouth and eyes are wet, and if her skin is not dry and wrinkled, you can rest assured that your baby is getting enough hindmilk. If you have any doubts that your baby is getting enough milk, it is important that you talk to your health-care provider.

A baby who isn't getting enough breast milk may not be nursing correctly, and a baby who isn't getting enough calories is probably not getting enough hindmilk, often due to mothers cutting feedings short. To make sure your baby takes in enough calories, allow him to nurse from the first breast until he is satisfied and drops off it by himself. If he's not interested in nursing on the other breast then, start with that one at the next feeding. This is called switch nursing.

A breastfeeding mother who is given instructions on proper positioning of her baby and how to get him to latch on to the breast has an easier time making sure her baby is getting just the right amount and quality of breast milk. Our book *The Breastfeeding Book* (Little, Brown, 2000) has illustrations and instructions on proper positioning and latch-on as well as advice on how to increase your milk supply. You can also get breastfeeding support and guidance from La Leche League International, which has chapters across the country (see Resources for Childcare Products and Information, page 133).

◌

DTP Shot: Safer for Baby

Q *My baby is scheduled to get his DTP shot, but my friends tell me that the pertussis portion of the vaccine can cause severe side effects in infants. Is this true? And if it is, should I not vaccinate my son?*

A Once upon a time infants did have adverse reactions to the pertussis vaccine (the P of the DTP shot, typically given in combination with diphtheria-tetanus toxoid), such as drowsiness, irritability, and high fever. There is now a new type of vaccine that protects infants against pertussis, or whooping cough, while causing fewer side effects. The acellular pertussis vaccine contains only parts of the pertussis bacterium and has routinely replaced the old whole-cell pertussis vaccine. While babies might still experience crankiness and low fever after receiving an a-DTP injection, such reactions are fewer and much less severe.

Pertussis is still a highly communicable and prevalent respiratory disease in children, causing inflammation of the lining of the airway passages, profuse mucus production, and a severe cough that can last for six weeks or more. Besides experiencing extreme discomfort and breathing difficulties—resulting in many sleepless nights for babies and their families—infants with whooping cough can also develop a secondary pneumonia and require hospitalization. Whooping cough is particularly serious in infants under one year of age.

With the current a-DTP vaccine, the benefits of immunization far outweigh the risks. We strongly suggest that you have your baby fully immunized according to the schedule recommended by the American Academy of Pediatrics, which includes an injection of a-DTP at two, four, and six months of age, followed by booster shots at eighteen months and five years.

☞

Ear Thermometers: Getting an Accurate Reading

Q *I use an ear thermometer to take my six-month-old's temperature, but I just read about a recent study that says ear thermometers may not be accurate. Should I forgo the ear thermometer altogether? What method gives the most accurate reading?*

A Like any device, ear thermometers are accurate only if they are used correctly. These easy-to-use thermometers record temperature by measuring the infrared rays radiating from the eardrum. The main problem with this type of thermometer is that to give an accurate reading, it needs to be pointed directly at the eardrum. If it's slanted, you will get a lower reading than the actual temperature. This is a particular problem with infants because their ear canals are so narrow. At your next doctor's visit, ask the nurse to show you how to use the thermometer correctly. If you take the temperature at least twice, you can rest assured you're getting a fairly accurate reading.

As a safeguard, get used to how your baby's normal temperature feels. Use your hands or your lips to touch the forehead or upper abdomen, the most accurate spots to register a temperature. We call this the "kiss and guess" method. Studies have shown that parents using this method are accurate 75 percent of the time in telling whether their baby has a temperature. Also, watch for these signs of fever: flushed cheeks, fast heartbeat, faster breathing with hot breath, and sweating.

When the ear thermometer registers normal but your senses tell you otherwise, take your baby's temperature rectally, which is the most accurate.

How your baby acts and looks is more important than the degree of your baby's fever. A higher fever does not always mean a sicker baby. In fact, some minor viral illnesses produce the highest fevers (104° to 105° F).

If your baby has a fever, you don't have to worry as long as he is playing normally, smiling and alert, and his skin is its normal color, other than perhaps flushed cheeks. But you should call your doctor immediately if your baby is under three months; acts sicker by the hour; becomes increasingly lethargic, drowsy, and less responsive; has a dull, anxious facial expression; or if his skin is pale or ashen. Also call your doctor if your baby seems no better when the fever subsides.

Fever is a symptom of an underlying illness, not an illness itself. It's a warning to pay attention, sort of like the warning light that goes on in your car to check your engine.

❦

A Newborn's Fingernails

Q *When is it okay to cut a newborn's fingernails for the first time? The hospital made it sound like I shouldn't cut them right away. My sister bit off her newborn's nails. Is that a good practice?*

A Although many newborns enter the world with fingernails long enough to scratch their adorable little faces, the hospital staff usually refuse to cut infants' fingernails, mainly for legal reasons in the event that a nurse clipped too deeply and cut an infant's finger. Instead, they ask parents to cut their baby's fingernails the day after leaving the hospital.

It's okay to bite off your newborn's nails, but there's an easier way. Wait until your baby is in a deep sleep, recognized by the limp-limb sign, when her limbs dangle limply at her side. Then cut her nails with a pair of nail clippers, preferably a set designed for babies.

To avoid snipping the fingertip skin as you clip the nail, depress the finger pad away from the nail as you cut. As a beginning nail cutter, have your spouse hold baby's hand while you manipulate the finger and the nail clipper. After a while you will be able to trim baby's nails by yourself.

Don't feel like a child abuser if you accidentally draw a few drops of blood. Every parent accidentally goes too deep at one time or another. A nail that was clipped too closely seldom gets infected, though it would be wise to apply an antibiotic ointment to the damaged skin for a few days afterward.

Newborn nails are soft and cut easily, but they grow quickly, so try to keep them trimmed as close as you possibly can. Toenails don't grow as fast and tend to be harder to get at without cutting baby. Don't cut them as often as you do the fingernails.

✑

Sleep Requirements for Children

Q *My thirteen-month-old daughter sleeps from 10:00 P.M. to 8:00 A.M. She also has two one-hour naps during the day. Is this enough sleep? How much sleep should a baby get at different ages?*

A Most thirteen-month-olds sleep twelve to fourteen hours a day, including naps, so your daughter is within the range. If she seems well rested, this may be enough sleep for her. If she seems tired or irritable or nods off to sleep frequently during that day, she needs more. Below is a chart of average sleeping times for children of different ages:

Age	Hours per Day
birth to 3 months	14 to 18
3 to 6 months	14 to 16
6 months to 2 years	12 to 14
2 to 5 years	10 to 12

A ten o'clock P.M. bedtime would once have been considered late for a thirteen-month-old. Modern lifestyles have pushed bedtimes later, especially among working couples, who might not get home until six or seven in the evening and prefer that their baby take a late-afternoon nap and be well rested for quality time in the evening. Some parents prefer the later bedtimes so that they can get that extra hour of sleep in the morning. Other parents want an earlier bedtime so that they can get in some baby-free couple time in the evening.

Use the bedtime that works best for you and your baby. If the 10:00 P.M. lights-out keeps your baby rested and suits your schedule, stay with it.

✺

The Baby-Tossing Game

Q *My husband likes to play with our twelve-month-old son by tossing him into the air and catching him. Baby Todd loves it! He giggles, laughs, and smiles to beat the band. But could this be dangerous? This can't result in shaken baby syndrome, can it?*

A Babies have survived being tossed by their parents without harm for centuries. Most parents intuitively know how to toss and catch their babies safely, despite the worried spectators who hover in the background.

Tossing and catching a baby is very different from

shaken baby syndrome, which occurs when a baby's head is violently shaken back and forth, resulting in bruising and bleeding of the brain and damaging of the spinal cord and eyes. When you toss and catch a baby, the baby is eased slowly out of your arms and returned gradually. Shaken baby syndrome involves more abrupt, sudden movements that bend the bones of the lower neck.

While babies under six months of age shouldn't be played with in this way, a twelve-month-old baby has enough head control and neck muscle strength to protect his head from injury during tossing. It is important, however, that Dad catch his baby in a standing position, vertically with support underneath both arms, as most baby tossers do. This way, the baby's head can't abruptly flip backward or forward. Next time your husband and baby are playing the tossing game, watch how your husband catches your baby and be sure that your baby comes down into his arms vertically, not lying horizontal. Also make sure that your husband catches your baby under both arms, keeping his head well supported.

❧

Help for Teethers

Q *My eight-month-old is teething right now, and anesthetic gels don't seem to be working. What can I do to help her out?*

A It can be very painful when those pearly whites come through sensitive gums. Contrary to popular expression, babies don't "cut" teeth; nor do their teeth "erupt." Rather, teeth slowly slide and twist their way through tender gum tissue. Not only does this hurt, but it can also cause excessive drooling.

Drooling in turn can lead to a rash on the chin and neck; a cough caused by excess saliva dripping down and irritating baby's throat; diarrhea or loose stools; a low-grade fever (101° F); night waking; and general crankiness. In addition, your little teether will continuously long for something (or someone!) to gnaw on, so give her something cool and hard. Avoid over-the-counter topical anesthetics since they have never been proven safe or effective for infants.

Gum-soothing favorites that have worked with our kids include a cool spoon, a cold washcloth, a Popsicle, a chilled rubber teething ring, a refrigerated teething biscuit, a frozen banana, or a frozen plain bagel.

You can also give your little one a dropper (0.8 milliliters) of acetaminophen (Tylenol) before bedtime to ease nighttime discomfort and help her sleep. Because new teeth tend to appear on average one a month until a child is around two years old, be prepared to make these pain-relieving rituals a monthly event!

The Aspirin–Reye's Syndrome Connection

Q *I have a four-year-old, and I worry about giving him aspirin because I've heard it can lead to Reye's syndrome. I understand that I shouldn't use aspirin when he has chicken pox or fever-related influenza. But what about simple aches and pains associated with fever or flu-like symptoms?*

A It has never been proven that giving aspirin to a child with chicken pox or influenza will cause Reye's syndrome, an inflammation of the brain and liver. However, there has been some evidence to suggest a connection of some kind, which should be enough to dissuade any parent from giving aspirin to his or her child.

Reye's syndrome is a very serious disease that affects children of all ages. It typically sets in about a week after an upper-respiratory infection or chicken pox. Symptoms include increasing lethargy that may lead to coma; persistent vomiting; and fever. Intensive care is a must as the syndrome often needs to be treated with intravenous fluids and Dexamethasone to reduce the swelling of the brain. About 20 percent of all cases end in death.

The exact cause of this disease is unknown, but it is thought that toxins released by a viral illness provoke a hypersensitive reaction by the liver, damaging it in the process. Reye's syndrome has been seen in many cases in which the child was given aspirin, so parents have been advised not to give aspirin to their children during a viral illness.

In our opinion, giving your child aspirin is simply not worth the risk (except for rheumatoidlike conditions, such as rheumatoid arthritis) since there are plenty of safer alternatives that are available over the counter. Use acetaminophen (Tylenol) and/or ibuprofen (Advil, Motrin) for fever management and ibuprofen as an anti-inflammatory.

$\mathscr{D}$

Traveling Overseas with Baby

Q *My husband and I are planning a trip to Chile when our son is between eight and ten months old. We've already talked to our pediatrician, who recommended a Hepatitis A immunization a week prior to departure. What are the health risks for a child this age traveling overseas?*

A Every country has different health risks and consequent recommendations, and they often change from month to month. For the most up-to-date information, you should call the Centers for Disease Control's International Travelers' Hotline toll-free at 877-FYI-TRIP or visit their Web site at www.cdc.gov and look for travelers' health information. In addition, I recommend drinking bottled water rather than tap water in any foreign country you are visiting.

Foreign disease shouldn't be your only concern when you travel. To make any plane trip (foreign or domestic) safer and more comfortable for the whole family, consider the following:

- If your baby is not used to being carried in a sling or other carrier, start using one now. These useful devices enable you to carry a small child through busy airports and crowds with minimal exposure to strangers.
- Book a no-smoking flight. There are still some international airlines that allow smoking. Tiny air passages are particularly sensitive to air pollution from cigarette smoke. Even if you're seated in the so-called no-smoking section of an aircraft, you're still going to inhale pollutants from the smoking section. (Think of it as trying to chlorinate half a swimming pool—it can't be done.)
- Nurse your baby or give him a bottle while the plane is ascending. Tiny ears are particularly sensitive to changes in altitude, and sucking on something will help prevent uncomfortable pressure from building up in his eustachian tubes. You might also consider waking your little one for a feeding when the plane begins to descend, too, since eustachian tubes don't adjust well to altitude changes while a baby's sleeping and may cause discomfort.
- Give your baby extra fluids to drink, since babies, like adults, can get dehydrated easily on long flights.
- Spritz your baby's nose with a saline nasal spray every few hours. The low humidity on planes is likely to make his tiny nose stuff up, so he'll appreciate the relief these sprays bring. (Look for them in small over-the-counter squirt bottles at your local pharmacy.)
- Request a bulkhead seat. In many cases, these seats are

equipped with pull-down bassinets and have extra floor space.

࿇

Late Teething

Q *My baby just turned one, and he still doesn't have any teeth. Should I be concerned?*

A   The timing of a baby's first tooth is as variable as when he takes his first steps. And as long as the rest of his developmental milestones are on schedule, you do not have to be concerned about late teething; it won't affect his health or result in teeth of lesser quality.

The one drawback to being a late teether is that your baby's teeth will probably arrive in clusters (two or three at a time), which means he'll probably have an extra dose of teething pain. And since teething tends to increase drooling, you can also expect a drool rash on his chin, especially if his sensitive skin ends up rubbing against a drool-soaked sheet at night. A drool cough is another common side effect, caused by excess saliva dripping down the back of baby's throat. Drool diarrhea can also occur, due to excess saliva entering the intestines. Finally, you can expect a low-grade fever (101° F) and irritability as hard teeth push through soft gums. For suggestions on easing teething discomfort, see page 95.

Incidentally, your baby actually has a full set of teeth already. They're just buried in his gums, waiting for the time to sprout. Exactly when that happens is partly deter-mined by heredity, so you might want to check your family tree to see if anyone else was a late teether.

✑

Sterilizing Baby Bottles

Q *My sister and I are debating whether baby bottles need to be sterilized. I say they do—for at least the first six months. My sister thinks sterilizing isn't necessary at all. Who's right?*

A You are. It's important to sterilize a baby's bottles for at least the first six months to protect against food-borne infections. This is because milk and formula residue is hard to remove and serves as a fertile breeding ground for germs that can cause diarrhea. For babies diarrhea is a serious condition because dehydration can happen so quickly in infancy.

Fortunately, sterilizing is quite simple. A dishwasher with a water temperature of at least 180° F will adequately clean and sterilize bottles and their accessories. If your sister doesn't have a dishwasher, encourage her to try the following procedure after washing the equipment in hot, soapy water and rinsing it thoroughly. Pad the bottom of a large pot with a clean towel or dishcloth (to avoid sticking or breakage), fill it with water, and immerse open bottles, nipples, and other equipment in the pot. Place bottles on their sides to be sure they get filled with the sterilizing water. Cover the pot and bring the water to a boil for ten minutes. Let everything cool to room temperature while the pot is still covered. Finally, remove the bottles and nipples with tongs or spoons, place the bottles upside down on a clean towel with the nipples and caps alongside, and let the equipment dry. Make sure the place where bottles are stored is kept clean and dry.

Circumcision

Q *Do you consider circumcision a necessary procedure? Are there any health advantages? I read somewhere that the benefits aren't as great as was once thought.*

A No part of an infant's body has stirred as much debate as the foreskin. Even the American Academy of Pediatrics (AAP) has gone back and forth on this issue. In 1989, prompted by research that showed a link between circumcision and a lower incidence of urinary tract infections (UTIs) and sexually transmitted diseases, the AAP concluded that the procedure did have medical benefits and advantages as well as risks. On March 1, 1999, the AAP reversed its recommendation, stating that the benefits of circumcision are not significant enough to recommend it as a routine procedure. The consensus among pediatricians is that there is no universal medical reason for routine circumcision.

While a few studies have suggested that the risk of

UTIs is higher in uncircumcised boys than in boys who are circumcised, these studies have been statistical in nature, and the foreskin hasn't been proven to be the cause of an increased occurrence of UTIs. Besides, UTIs are rare in males, circumcised or not. Research indicates that during the first year of life an uncircumcised male infant has at most a 1 in 100 chance of developing a UTI, while a circumcised male has about a 1 in 1,000 chance.

Research has also found that the risk of an uncircumcised man developing penile cancer is more than three times that of a circumcised man. However, penile cancer is extremely rare, with only nine to ten cases diagnosed per one million men each year. Studies have also suggested that circumcised men may be at a reduced risk for developing syphilis and HIV infections, but behavioral factors are the most important determinant of whether a man is at risk of contracting a sexually transmitted disease.

That being the case, the question of whether to circumcise your son is largely a personal decision, and for some people a cultural or religious issue. While circumcision was once considered a routine procedure for newborn males in the United States, more and more parents are now questioning its necessity.

Here are some facts to consider when deciding whether or not to circumcise your baby:

- *Surgical risks.* Circumcision is usually a very safe surgical procedure. Yet, as with any surgical procedure, there is the rare problem of bleeding, infection, or injury to the penis.
- *Pain.* The circumcision procedure hurts. The myth that newborns do not feel pain during circumcision came from the fact that newborns sometimes withdraw into a deep sleep toward the end of the operation. But this is

actually a retreat mechanism, a withdrawal reaction to overwhelming pain. Studies have since shown that during unanesthetized circumcision, stress hormones rise, the heart rate speeds up, and the oxygen content of the baby's blood diminishes. The AAP's recommendation is that if parents decide to circumcise their infant, pain relief must be provided.

Most doctors today perform circumcision using a local anesthetic. If you choose to circumcise your infant, insist that it be done under local anesthesia. The most common and effective method is called a dorsal penile nerve block, in which a few drops of Xylocaine (similar to the anesthetic your dentist uses) are injected into the nerves on each side of the penis. This seldom relieves all the pain of circumcision, but in most cases it significantly reduces it.

- *Rationale.* Keep in mind that being different isn't bad. Having a baby circumcised just so he won't feel different from his friends isn't a good enough reason to go ahead with the procedure. The percentage of intact males has risen steadily in recent years and is probably about fifty-fifty nationwide by now. Locker-room comparisons and the "like father, like son" feeling are outdated—few fathers and sons compare foreskins.

The circumcision debate is likely to continue for years, even as routine circumcision becomes a thing of the past. It's up to each family to decide what is right for their child.

◌⃟

Baby Spit-Up

Q *My six-month-old son spits up a lot. Nothing seems to help. Could there be something seriously wrong with him?*

A Many infants spit up without having an underlying medical problem. In fact, spit-up is usually more of a laundry problem than a health one. In partnership with your doctor, consider these possibilities:

- *Overfeeding.* One general remedy for just about all gastrointestinal problems is smaller, more frequent meals. In other words, feed your baby less food more often. This makes sense when you consider that babies have tiny tummies—only a bit larger than their fists. If you place an 8-ounce bottle next to your baby's fist, you'll see what a challenge it is to get that much food into his little belly.

- *Gastroesophageal reflux (GER).* Around one-third of infants (especially boys) have some degree of reflux (see pages 13–14). This is perfectly normal, and most outgrow it by the time they are eight months old, when they learn to sit upright so gravity can hold the milk and food down. In the meantime, besides offering smaller, more frequent meals, you can help minimize GER by keeping your baby upright and quiet for half an hour after each feeding. In some cases, your doctor may decide to treat your baby with medicine that neutralizes the stomach acid and/or accelerates the time it takes for food to go from the stomach into the intestines.

- *Formula or food allergy.* Your doctor can help you discover if this is causing your baby's spit-up. You may have to experiment with different formulas.
- *Incorrect size of nipple hole.* If you bottlefeed, make sure the nipple hole is large enough that the formula drips out one drop per second (test it by holding a bottle upside down without shaking it). If baby has to work too hard to get the milk out, he may swallow a lot of air in the process and spit up as a result.

That having been said, do alert your doctor if your baby exhibits any of the following signs, since they may indicate a problem that requires medical attention:

- Baby is losing weight or not gaining weight sufficiently.
- Baby is spitting up more and more frequently, in greater and greater amounts, and the spit-up has become "projectile" (it flies across your lap and onto the floor).
- The spit-up is consistently green (which indicates the presence of bile, a liquid produced by the liver to aid digestion).
- Baby acts colicky and appears to be in pain when he spits up.
- Baby gags and coughs during every feeding.

*

Lyme Disease

Q *I read that there's a new Lyme disease vaccine. Should my kids get inoculated?*

A Lyme disease gets its name because it was discovered in Lyme, Connecticut. It is caused by the *Borrelia burgdorferi* bacterium carried by deer ticks and is transmitted to humans through tick bites. A red rash usually develops around the tick bite site between seven and fourteen days after the bite but could develop anywhere between three and thirty-one days later. After that come flu-like symptoms: fatigue, chills, fever, joint pain, muscle aches, and headaches. Arthritis may also occur. If the disease goes untreated, it can affect the nerves or the heart and can even result in chronic arthritis, heart disease, or, in rare cases, damage to the central nervous system. A primary diagnosis can be made upon the appearance of the rash and confirmed with a blood test. It is usually successfully treated with antibiotics.

Although there have been cases reported in all fifty states, the disease is seen primarily in the Northeast (from Massachusetts to Maryland) and the upper Midwest (especially in Wisconsin and Minnesota), and sometimes on the West Coast (particularly in northern California).

Lyme disease gets a lot of press, but after almost thirty years in pediatrics, I'm still waiting to see my first case. It is, however, an illness that you should be aware of just in case your child is bitten by a tick and develops the symptoms described above.

The Lyme disease vaccine, called LYMErix, which is applied in three doses over the course of a year, hasn't been approved for children younger than fifteen. It is 80 percent effective against the disease after the third dose. But even if your children happen to be old enough to receive the vaccination, Lyme disease is extremely rare, so I think routine vaccination is unnecessary. On the other hand, if you live in an area where the disease is prevalent, or if you plan to do a lot of hiking or camping in such a place, you might consider having your older children, or perhaps all family members over fourteen, inoculated.

The best tactic against Lyme disease is to avoid tick-infested areas. But if that is impossible, try these preventive measures:

- Dress in clothes that cover your arms and legs.
- Tuck pants into boots and button long-sleeve shirts at the cuff.
- Apply tick and insect repellents (sparingly) to the skin every couple of hours. Be sure to wash your child's skin as soon as he comes indoors to keep him from absorbing too many of the toxins.
- If a tick bites your child, remove it promptly. Avoid squeezing the body of the tick. Grasp the tick's body with tweezers close to the skin and remove it by gently pulling the tick straight out (without twisting). Take the tick to your doctor for identification if you think it may be carrying Lyme disease.

Despite its reputation, Lyme disease is pretty rare, so if you take these precautions, you and your child will probably never contract it.

☙

Cold Busters

Q *Last winter our seventeen-month-old boy suffered from constant colds with phlegm and high fever. He was treated with antibiotics. Now our son has caught his first cold of the season with identical symptoms. Are there any preventive guidelines, including alternative medicine, that we can follow?*

A Most babies come down with six to eight colds during their first two years. Colds interfere with a baby's sleep, cause parents to miss work, and cause doctors to get phone calls. You are wise to want to avoid the need for antibiotics, but be prepared for your baby to need antibiotics at least a couple of times a year during the first three years.

The saying "to catch cold" is medically accurate, but it's even more correct to say the cold catches the child. Cold germs travel by droplets—microscopic water balloons that are tossed into the air by a cough or sneeze and then inhaled by another person within cold-catching distance. These droplets and their germ passengers also travel from hand to hand. So not only can we catch a cold, we can literally pick one up. Baby A rubs her snotty nose with her hands and touches Baby B with her gooey hand. Then Baby B rubs his nose, and the germs find a new home.

Here are some simple preventive measures that keep colds from progressing into ear infections or bronchitis and may alleviate the need for antibiotics:

• *Limit exposure.* To minimize the spread of germs, limit your baby's exposure to children with obvious colds. If

your child is in day care, be sure the center has a strin-
gent policy of not admitting sick kids. If the frequency
and severity of your baby's colds continue, you may
have to reassess baby's day-care situation.
- *Wash your child's hands after he wipes his nose or
coughs.*
- *Teach your baby the "cold shoulder technique."* When
he needs to cough or sneeze, show him how to turn his
head toward his shoulder while lifting his arm in front of
his face, instead of covering his nose and mouth with his
hands. Coughing into the shoulder or upper arm spreads
fewer germs than coughing into the hands.
- *Hose the nose.* Most children less than three years old
have difficulty blowing their noses, so you must do it for
them. Buy saline nasal spray, a specially formulated saltwater mist solution available over the counter. Or make
your own saltwater solution (no more than ¼ teaspoon
of salt dissolved in an 8-ounce glass of warm water).
Squirt some solution into each nostril. Then lay baby
down for a minute with his head lower than his body.
This allows the saltwater to loosen the thick secretions
and stimulates baby to sneeze them to the front of the
nose. You can then grab the thick stuff with your trusty
nasal aspirator (or "snot snatcher"), available at your
pharmacy. You can teach your baby to blow his own
nose by the time he is three years of age. Teach him to
blow out a candle and then show him how to do it with
his nose. Remember, the nose is the point of entry for
germs to invade the rest of the respiratory passages (the
ears and bronchial tubes). So keeping the nose germ-free
will lessen your baby's need for antibiotics.
- *Thin the secretions.* During a cold, thick mucus accumu-
lates in baby's breathing passages and acts as a culture
medium for bacteria. Thinning the mucus will prevent

bacteria from accumulating. To do this, give baby extra fluids during the day and run a warm-mist vaporizer while he sleeps. Also, steam clean your baby's nasal passages by carrying him into a steamy shower. Steam opens clogged breathing passages and helps drain the secretions.

Mole Patrol

Q *My twenty-two-month-old son was born with a small flat mole on his back. It continues to grow as he does, but the color and shape haven't changed. Are moles like this common and are they dangerous? Will it continue to grow and should it be removed?*

A Moles on children are seldom a problem. They rarely become cancerous and usually fade with time. But be sure to mention this mole to your doctor at each of your child's checkups. As your child gets older, look for the following signs that the mole may need medical attention: the color becomes deeper and more irregular; the otherwise smooth borders become more irregular.

Finger Sucking

Q *My three-year-old sucks her fingers when she's tired, hungry, or bored. Her lips are split, and she has a callus on her middle finger. At what point should I be concerned, and how do I get her to stop?*

A Many children use their fingers and thumbs as a pacifier (which literally means "peacemaker") to reduce stress. Finger sucking is more dental friendly than thumb sucking, so you don't have to worry that it will harm her teeth. You can lessen this harmless habit by keeping those little hands busy. As soon as you see the hands and mouth searching for each other, give your youngster an activity to do that requires the use of her hands. For example, teach her that as soon as she feels like sucking her finger she should instead grab her finger and talk to it, or grab her sleeve, or hold on to a favorite toy that she can carry around in her pocket.

Try not to take your daughter's finger-sucking habit personally or worry that she lacks attention or has an emotional disturbance. Many well-adjusted children use their body parts to simply self-soothe. To get rid of these annoying little habits of childhood, use the "distract and substitute" method: Distract her from her habit and substitute a more acceptable one.

☙

Urinary Tract Infections in Boys

Q *I have a twenty-one-month-old son who was diag-nosed with a urinary tract infection. I thought UTIs affected mostly girls, and I'm curious about how he got the infection. We change his diaper every four hours and take good care of him. Could eating food with sodium be the cause? I'd also like to know what antibiotic is commonly used to treat UTIs.*

A You are correct that urinary tract infections usually affect girls. In light of this, a urinary tract infection in a male infant needs to be taken more seriously. When a baby boy contracts a UTI, it usually indicates a structural abnormality in the kidneys or bladder, which, if not cor-rected, could predispose the child to more infections and subsequent kidney damage. For this reason, your doctor will probably want to pursue a more extensive evaluation, such as a renal ultrasound and further X-ray studies, to be sure that your child's urinary tract drainage is free of struc-tural problems.

Urinary tract infections have nothing to do with how well you care for your child. Eating food with sodium also does not cause a urinary tract infection (though too much salt in a child's diet can cause the urine to become too con-centrated, leading to a diaper rash). At your son's age, sulfa (Septra or Bactrim) is a commonly used antibiotic for uri-nary tract infections. We suggest that you discuss a thor-ough kidney investigation with your pediatrician.

◌

Baby Lumps

Q *Recently I discovered a small lump on the right side of my two-month-old son's neck. Our doctor said it was just a swollen lymph node, which is common in newborns. What causes these lumps, and should I be concerned?*

A As your doctor said, this is a normal lymph node or gland. In fact, get used to feeling lots of lumps on your growing baby's body.

During the first three months, babies normally develop many pea-size lymph glands, noticeable primarily on the back of the head, the nape of the neck, and along the sides of the neck beneath the jaw. You will also normally feel these glands in your baby's armpits and groin. These glands help the body's defense mechanisms in fighting germs and are important to a baby's developing immune system.

From time to time you may notice that some lymph nodes swell to larger than usual size. This can happen if your baby has an infection anywhere near the glands, such as in the throat or ears. Even an insignificant scratch on the scalp can cause the nearby lymph glands to swell.

We teach new parents in our pediatrics practice to be keen observers and accurate reporters on their babies. Get to know your baby's body well so that you are accustomed to the normal size and feel of these glands. If you notice any changes in the glands, report them to your pediatrician at your baby's next routine checkup so that your doctor can evaluate your concerns.

Get the Facts on Prescriptions

Q *I heard on the news that the prescription information fliers distributed by pharmacists are often outdated or
inaccurate. As a parent, this terrifies me. I don't like giving
my kids medication as it is, but now I have to wonder
whether the drugs could have harmful side effects. I try to
be a good parent, and I try to read the patient information
leaflets, but how do I guarantee that a prescribed drug
won't hurt my kids?*

A   The ultimate responsibility for drug information and
safety rests with the physician who prescribes the drug.
When your child's doctor prescribes a medication, ask
about side effects you should be aware of and watch for.
And if your child is on other drugs, make sure to ask
whether it's safe to take them together.

A recent study by a consumer advocacy group called
Public Citizen found instances in which patient information leaflets (PILs) were misleading or failed to include
important information. The group called on the U.S. Food
and Drug Administration to recall PILs that contain potentially harmful inaccuracies.

No one argues that the PILs should be accurate and up-
to-date, but as a safeguard it's always a good idea to compare that information with the advice you get from your
doctor and pharmacist. It's also helpful to read the prescription yourself, repeating the instructions aloud to your
doctor ("So I should give her one teaspoon three times a

day for seven days"). This way you'll leave the office knowing the dosage, frequency, and duration of the medication.

When the prescription's filled, make sure it matches your understanding of the doctor's order. Read the label and compare it with what the doctor told you. If there's a question, check with the doctor.

Sometimes pharmacists alter prescriptions to make the medicine easier to administer, possibly supplying a higher concentration of a drug to reduce the dosage. Again, if the prescription label is different from what you expected, ask the pharmacist to clarify.

Remember, the best source of information on any prescription is your doctor. And if you don't understand any aspect of your child's treatment, you shouldn't be afraid to ask.

✍

Asthma

Q *My three-year-old daughter saw her doctor today because she was wheezing, coughing, and crying. The doctor thinks the problem is related to a virus that may lead to asthma. She was on a breathing machine and is currently taking Ventolin. Is this common, and is it likely to lead to asthma? Also, are there any signs to watch out for in the meantime?*

A Don't let the term "asthma" scare you. Asthma simply means wheezing, and many preschool children wheeze in reaction to a virus. When a virus strikes, the breathing passage airways becoming inflamed, causing the muscles of the trachea and bronchi to go into spasms. Most children outgrow the tendency to wheeze following a virus and do not develop what you would call "asthma." If there is no strong family history of allergic asthma, your child is unlikely to become asthmatic.

When your daughter gets her next cold, these preventive measures should keep it from going into her chest and causing her to wheeze:

- Get her to rest. Relaxing her mind and body will also relax her airways, making her less likely to wheeze.
- Prop her up at a 45-degree angle when she's in bed.
- Hose the nose. Use a warm-mist vaporizer and flush the nose frequently with saline nasal spray, available over the counter or in a homemade version (see page 8). Keeping the nose clear of secretions lessens the chances of the germs traveling down into the lower airways.
- Steam clean her nose by carrying her into a steamy shower. Steam opens clogged breathing passages and helps drain the secretions.
- When your child has a mucus-producing cough, clap on her chest to dislodge mucus plugs that may become trapped in the airways and trigger a wheeze. (Ask your doctor to show you how to do this.)
- Allergy-proof your child's sleeping environment by getting rid of dust collectors (feather pillows, down comforters, and fuzzy toys).

Potty Training Regression

Q *My twenty-three-month-old daughter initiated her own potty training after watching her twin older brothers (age three and a half) learning to use the potty. For three weeks she told me when she needed to go, and she rarely had accidents. Now she has regressed and has started having frequent potty accidents. I suspect this is normal, but I'm not sure if I should just roll with it or put her back in diapers.*

A With major developmental milestones such as toilet training, it's normal for children to take two steps forward and one step backward. Progressions and regressions like the one you describe with your daughter's potty training are common. Our advice is to encourage your child when she makes progress and to roll with it when she regresses.

On an added note, because of their anatomy, girls are more prone to urinary tract infections than boys. Therefore, it is important for your daughter to learn to pay attention to her bladder signals—to go when her body tells her she needs to. Ignoring these body signals and holding on to urine could predispose her to bladder infections. If your child isn't able to attend to these signals and if you're both getting stressed over it, it's certainly okay to put her back in diapers and give it more time.

❧

First Trip to the Dentist

Q *When should a child begin going to the dentist? My three-year-old twins are uncooperative and won't allow me to brush their teeth. Should I schedule an appointment anyway?*

A Children should have a dental exam between two and three years of age, after all of their first teeth have come in. Even if your dentist is unable to examine every tooth during the initial visit, your youngsters will meet him or her, and you'll receive helpful information on preventive hygiene. To prepare your children for the event, explain ahead of time what to expect during their first appointment. Let the dentist examine the twins together; if one twin is more cooperative, she can be a model for her more reluctant sibling.

Here are some strategies that encourage tooth-brushing:

- *Brush together.* Let your children copy your brushing techniques.
- *Make it fun.* Teach them how to play "let's wash off the sugar bugs" and other brushing games.
- *Use incentives,* such as reading a story after they finish brushing their teeth.
- *Try the two-parent tooth-brushing method.* Mom and Dad sit facing each other (knee-to-knee), the child lies across their laps, and one parent brushes the child's teeth from above.

☙

Two Safety Seats, One Safe Spot

Q *As the parent of two-year-old twin boys, how do I place two car seats in the car safely when the safest spot is in the middle of the backseat? This is a big concern to me. Please help!*

A As concerned parents like you realize, raising healthy children extends to ensuring their personal safety, including in the car. The safest place for one child in a car seat is in the middle of the backseat, as this is the area of the car that is furthest from any potential impact. With a baby in a safety seat in the backseat, some drivers may be tempted to take their eyes off the road to check on the child, so get used to glancing very quickly in the rearview mirror to check on your child and pull over safely if your child needs attention.

Driving with two active toddlers in car seats is a bit challenging. Putting your second child behind your seat both exposes him to the risk of injury from the side and might tempt you to take your eyes off the road to turn around to check on him. Placing him on the passenger side in the backseat lets you see him more easily but exposes him to the risk of injury from side impact. However, either spot in the backseat is less risky than the front seat. The front seat passenger side (the most dangerous location in a car) exposes the child to the risk of both front and side impact and to the danger of suffocation from an inflated passenger-side airbag (if one is installed in your car). Placing a child in the middle of the front seat is also dan-

gerous if there is a head-on collision that causes the driver
and passenger-side airbags to inflate, especially if your car
does not have a wide bench-type front seat.

So you are left with two active children in the backseat
in separate car seats, one in the middle and one on the passenger side. As they grow, this may result in excessive sibling squabbling, but at least they will be safe. An ideal
solution simply doesn't exist, so you just have to do whatever you can to lower their risk of injury.

꧁

Finding the Perfect Pediatrician

Q *How do I find a pediatrician who shares the views
you express in this book?*

A The ideal pediatrician is both medically competent
and supportive of your parenting style. But finding one can
be a challenge, since many pediatricians are overly concerned about spoiling children and advocate forced early
independence. Ask friends with similar parenting styles
whom they use for pediatric care and what they think
about the quality of care they receive. If you can't find a
doctor who supports your parenting style, choose one who
is medically competent and seek parenting support else-
where. Many mothers find the support they need through
La Leche League or other national and local groups; some
even organize their own mothers' groups.

As your confidence in your child-rearing judgment grows, it won't be as crucial for you and your pediatrician to see eye-to-eye on every major parenting decision. And as your doctor-patient relationship develops, your thriving child will be the best measure of your success as a parent. A pediatrician who sees a healthy parent-child relationship usually supports what the parent is doing rather than giving advice that might prove counter-productive.

⁂

Solving the Mystery of Food Allergies

Q *My two-year-old daughter has wheezed off and on since she was an infant. She also has rashes and a frequent runny nose. She has been on soy formula for most of her life, but to no avail. Now our pediatrician wants to try her on a new inhaled steroid, which is put in her nebulizer to help calm the inflammation. Do you agree? Will the inhaled steroid hurt her in any way?*

A It certainly sounds like your child has multiple allergies, as your pediatrician suspects. The most likely culprits are inhalants (dust, pollens, animal dander, and cigarette smoke) or foods (dairy products, chocolate, egg whites, shellfish, tomatoes, wheat, berries, and nuts).

Inhaling steroids, if closely monitored by your child's

doctor, is one of the most effective ways to prevent recurrent wheezing. It's certainly safer to inhale steroids than to take them orally. But even inhaled steroids, if overused, can interfere with your child's normal growth. To reduce the allergy, try the following preventive measures: First, in cooperation with your pediatrician and allergist, figure out what you detect to be the most obvious allergens. Then allergy-proof your home. To track down hidden inhalant allergies, begin by "defuzzing" your toddler's bedroom. You should suspect she's allergic to something in her bedroom if she has frequent night coughs and awakens in the morning with a stuffy nose. Try to maintain a dust-free sleeping environment for your child using the following steps:

- Remove fuzzy stuffed toys from your child's crib or bed.
- Use a nonallergenic mattress, and cover the mattress with special dust-proof covers.
- Avoid fuzzy bedding, wool blankets, and down comforters.
- Wash the linens frequently.
- Keep the windows to your child's bedroom closed during hayfever season. Wash her hair nightly before bed to remove any pollens collected during the day.
- Use a HEPA-type air filter in her bedroom to remove dust and pollen.
- If you highly suspect bedroom allergies, remove wall-to-wall carpet and place washable throw rugs on wood or linoleum.
- Clean and replace air filters frequently, especially if you have a forced-air heating system.
- Keep all pets out of your child's bedroom.

While skin and blood tests may help to detect the most likely food allergens, your observations are the most reliable evidence. Rarely do food allergies cause wheezing alone. They also cause skin rashes and intestinal symptoms, such as bloating, diarrhea, or abdominal pain.

To help track down hidden food allergies, put your child on an elimination diet by taking away the most common food allergens for a week. First eliminate dairy products, wheat, egg whites, nuts, chocolate, corn, and citrus fruits. After a week on the elimination diet, reintroduce the eliminated foods into your child's diet. Do this very slowly, one food at a time every four days. You may start with a tiny bite or taste of the food. If there is no reaction, you can increase the amount you give your child. If any allergic symptoms reappear, you may surmise that a certain food is probably the primary cause. This food should go on your child's list of forbidden foods. Most food-allergic children can tolerate small portions of these foods if they eat them infrequently (every four days, on a sort of rotation diet).

It's important for you to chart your allergic child's progress. You are a VIP on your child's medical team. Your child's pediatrician and/or allergist will ask for your opinion on what your child is allergic to and how much the food is bothering her. As you proceed through the elimination diet, they will need to know if her allergies are getting better or worse. Since there is a fine line between over- and undertreatment of allergies in children, your child's doctor will base the extent of treatment on the history you present. Be a keen observer and an accurate reporter.

⌒

Understanding Failure to Thrive

Q *My son was adopted at age nine months. We were told that his birth mother neglected him, and when he was two months old, he had not gained weight and was diagnosed in the hospital with "failure to thrive." He then went into foster care and began to develop. Now he is three, but his speech and fine-motor development are delayed. I'm worried that this "failure to thrive" could have affected him permanently. Is that possible? Can you explain this to me?*

A   Your adopted child is blessed to now have a permanent home with caring parents. The "failure to thrive" that your child experienced during his early months of neglect is not necessarily permanent. Growing children need a lot of affection, touch, and responsiveness to their needs in order to thrive, and "thriving" means more than just gaining weight and growing taller. It means growing to one's full potential—physically, intellectually, and emotionally. Obviously, your son did not get this level of care in his previous home and therefore wasn't thriving. Now he's in a home that can provide the care he needs, and he should thrive.

Through the years as parents and in our pediatrics practice, we have noticed a phenomenon we call the "need-level concept." This means that all children are born with a certain level of need. If that need is fulfilled, they thrive. If that need is ignored, they don't thrive.

The key to helping your child thrive is to determine his particular level of need. Does he have a high need for touch, affection, love, attention, and/or interaction? Here are some specific suggestions that you can use to help him catch up in his development and begin to thrive:

- *Respond to his needs.* Research has shown that one of the most important determinants of a child's ability to thrive is the responsiveness of his caregivers to his cues. This does not mean giving your child everything he wants but rather everything he needs. When he gives a cue, such as wanting to play or wanting to be held, listen to him. In many cases infants who fail to thrive have learned that no one will listen to their cues, so they are not motivated to give their caregivers cues to what they need. This may be why your son's speech is delayed.

- *Be sure he has adequate nutrition.* Children need a well-balanced diet with a lot of protein, complex carbohydrates, and healthy fats (such as omega 3's, found in fish and vegetable oils). Nutritional deprivation, especially of proteins and healthy fats, can delay a child's development. If he doesn't like coldwater fish (salmon and tuna), give him a DHA supplement called Neuromins, an omega-3 fat that is vital for brain development.

- *Spend a lot of cuddle time with him,* even letting him fall asleep in your arms. Human touch is a wonderful way to stimulate development.

- *Give him a lot of eye-to-eye contact.* Most infants who suffer from a failure to thrive are withdrawn. Get him comfortable with looking at you when he speaks by saying, "I need your ears; I need your eyes."

- *Discover his special talent,* whether it be music, art, or sports. When a child excels in one area in life it carries over to his general sense of self-esteem.

Keep in mind that the neuromotor system of a developing child is amazingly resilient and can catch up from the delayed development as a result of early neglect. If you continue to make him feel wanted, loved, and cared for, you will see his development blossom.

☙

Treating Sneezing and Wheezing

Q *My two-year-old son has a long history of ear infections, sinusitis, and bronchitis. Lately when he gets bronchitis, he begins to wheeze. The doctor gave us Prednisone and albuterol to help open up his bronchial tubes. I get so nervous when he has these attacks. Isn't there a better way to treat the wheeze and bronchial asthma? I am afraid he's going to choke to death.*

A Wheezing following bronchitis or any other upper-respiratory infection is termed "infection-induced asthma." Another term you may hear for this condition is "reactive airway disease," or RAD. The muscular tissue in your child's bronchial tubes reacts to allergens and infections by narrowing and going into spasms. When the air passages narrow, this causes wheezing.

Prednisone and albuterol are medications that keep the airways from being so hyperreactive to allergens and infections. Besides these two medications, remember the best medicine is preventive. Try to identify what's triggering the wheeze. Do some detective work to determine the allergens, such as pollens, animal dander, or house dust. Above all, allergy-proof your child's bedroom as outlined on page 122.

Many children with RAD will wheeze when they exercise. This is called exercise-induced asthma. In this case, he may not be able to sprint and may need to temporarily limit strenuous exercise. As children get older, many with exercise-induced wheezing can perform quite well in competitive sports by simply taking a puff of an albuterol inhaler before the game.

Stress and anxiety can also trigger a wheeze. A relaxed child has relaxed airways. As soon as you detect a wheeze coming on, immediately click into a calming activity, such as reading a story, watching a video, or singing a song; oftentimes you can prevent the wheeze from getting serious enough to interfere with breathing.

What causes your son to choke are the mucus plugs that collect in the infected and inflamed airway. A golden rule of airway treatment is to keep secretions thin and moving. Give him fluids to drink. In my pediatrics practice I tell parents to give their wheezing child a good steam clean. Let him stand in the bathroom with a steamy shower or in front of a vaporizer for about twenty minutes until he can breathe easier.

Be sure to keep his nose cleaned out during colds. If the upper airway is clean and open, the lower airway tends to wheeze less. Also, build up his immunity by feeding him a variety of fresh fruits and vegetables.

Lastly, the good news is that unlike allergic wheezing, most children outgrow infection-induced wheezing and RAD.

Ꙅ

GER and Asthma

Q *My one-year-old baby, who has GER, wakes up coughing. The pediatrician said GER can cause asthma-like symptoms. How can that be? Does she have asthma and GER? What is the treatment for this?*

A Gastroesophageal reflux (GER) is caused by a malfunction of the valvelike muscles between the stomach and esophagus. Normally when food enters the stomach, the muscular band at the top of the stomach closes like a valve, keeping stomach acids and food contents from going back up. When this valve is weak, the food and irritating stomach acids reflux back up the esophagus, causing pain (colic and night waking) similar to what adults would call heartburn. Also, the regurgitated stomach contents in the esophagus and throat trigger a reflux that causes the airways to go into spasm, resulting in an asthma-like wheeze. Remember, the term "asthma" simply means wheezing. This can be triggered by an allergy, infection, or irritation such as GER.

Besides using doctor-prescribed medications that neutralize the stomach acids and accelerate the emptying of the stomach contents to lessen GER, here are some home remedies that you can try:

- Keep your child upright and quiet for at least thirty minutes after feeding.
- Offer smaller, more frequent feedings. As a general rule

feed her half as much twice as often. Feed her what are called rapid-transit foods. These foods (for example, smoothies, pureed foods, low-fat foods, fruits, and greens) empty from the stomach quickly. High-fat foods (such as those served at fast-food restaurants) stay in the stomach longer and are therefore regurgitated more.

• If you are still breastfeeding, continue to do so. Breast milk is known as the easy-in-easy-out food. It's easier to digest and empties twice as fast as cow's milk, so it's less likely to be regurgitated.

Most infants outgrow GER completely by one year of age. Pediatricians often advise parents, "Expect your child to walk out of her GER." Once children begin walking and spending most of their day upright, their GER subsides.

⚮

Symptoms of Pinkeye

Q *My three-year-old came home from his play group with a note saying that pinkeye was going around and to watch for certain symptoms. What is pinkeye? Is it contagious? What is the treatment?*

Pinkeye (the medical term is "conjunctivitis") is an inflammation of the white part of the eyeball, which is called the conjunctiva. The redness (or in this case pinkness) is caused by dilated blood vessels that branch over the white of the eyeball. The eye itches, burns, and is often sensitive to light. You may also notice a yellow discharge coming from beneath swollen eyelids.

The term "pinkeye" is a catch-all term for red eyes. Still, it's important to diagnose the cause in order to treat the child properly. If the conjunctivitis is caused by bacteria, the eyes have a yellow-green crust and the eyelids are usually swollen. When the conjunctivitis is caused by a virus, the eyes are very red, but there is little or no yellow drainage and both eyes are usually affected. Allergic conjunctivitis is usually seasonal, mostly in the spring. Both eyes are red and itchy, with no yellow drainage, although the eyes may be watery. During sunny summer months, some children get red eyes from sun irritation and/or irritation from the chlorine in swimming pools.

Allergen or irritant-induced conjunctivitis is not contagious, and a child can attend preschool or day care with it. But bacterial and viral conjunctivitis are contagious. They are spread by contact with the eyes when fingers rub infected eyes and share these germs with other children.

Bacterial conjunctivitis is easily treated with antibiotic eyedrops. Generally your child is no longer contagious forty-eight hours after beginning antibiotic eyedrop treatments. Even if the eyes are still red, once the yellow drainage has subsided (sometimes within a day of beginning treatment), you can consider your child no longer contagious.

As a final tip, if your child is a nose picker and eye rubber, discourage this habit. It is a common way of transferring the germs that live in the nose to the eyes.

☙

Nursemaid's Elbow

Q *My toddler came home from day care, and as I was giving her a bath, she would not let me wash her arm. While it did not seem to hurt her a great deal, she would not use this arm the next day and favored the other arm. I took her to our pediatrician, who diagnosed her with nursemaid's elbow. What is this, and how does it happen? I feel so guilty for letting her out of my care and haven't gone back to work for two weeks.*

A This common and harmless quirk is simply a pulled elbow. Suddenly jerking a young child's outstretched arm can easily cause a temporary dislocation of the arm bone out of the elbow joint. Following a sudden jerk on a child's arm, the arm hangs limp at the child's side and she refuses to use it, although it usually does not cause pain. A child may also protect her elbow by holding her arm bent across her chest as if it were in a sling. Sometimes the arm will slip back into the elbow joint on its own, but it usually requires manipulation by a doctor to painlessly pop it back in.

In your child's case, it probably occurred when another child tugged on her arm or a caregiver held or swung your child by one arm during play. In our pediatrics practice, we also call this the "come along Johnny" condition, since it can happen when someone takes a child's arm to get him to come quickly or to keep him from darting into the street.

You can prevent pulled elbows by picking up your child

by both arms, not swinging her by one arm, and not jerking her outstretched arm. By five years of age the ligaments of the child's elbow joint are stronger, so pulled elbows are rare.

After your doctor manipulates the arm bone back into the elbow joint it's important to allow the stretched ligaments to heal by placing the child's arm in a sling for a couple of days. You don't need to feel guilty or responsible for this problem, since it is a very common developmental quirk caused by the loose and elastic ligaments of the growing child. Once the arm bone is reset into the elbow joint, there is no permanent damage.

☙

Resources for Childcare Products and Information

Parenting and Pediatric Information

www.parenting.com. An informative Web site on parenting issues. Dr. Bill and Martha Sears answer parenting questions and host frequent chats and workshops.

www.askdrsears.com. A comprehensive Web site on healthcare information for infants and children.

Baby Carriers

A soft baby carrier is one of the most useful parenting products you and your baby will enjoy. Consult the following resources for information on sling-type carriers and step-by-step instructions on using a sling.

The Original BabySling
800-421-0526 or www.originalbabysling.com or www.nojo.com

Crown Crafts Infant Products
310-763-8100 or www.crowncraftsinfantproducts.com

www.AskDrSears.com   Visit our store.

Bedside Co-Sleepers

A bedside co-sleeper lets baby and parents sleep close to one another yet still have their own space. This criblike bed safely attaches to the parents' bed.

Arm's Reach Co-Sleeper 800-954-9353 or 818-879-9353 or www.armsreach.com

Nursing Clothing and Accessories

Motherwear 800-950-2500 or www.motherwear.com

Breastfeeding Help and Resources

La Leche League International (LLLI) 800-435-8316 or 847-519-7730 or www.lalecheleague.org

International Lactation Consultant Association (ILCA) 919-787-5181 or www.ilca.org

Corporate Lactation Program by Medela 800-435-8316 or www.medela.com

Attachment Parenting International 615-298-4334 or www.attachmentparenting.org

Mothering Multiples

National Organization of Mothers of Twins Clubs, Inc. 877-540-2200 or 615-595-0936 or www.nomotc.org

Index

Urinary tract infection (UTI),
33
  antibiotic for, 112
  in boys, 112
  circumcision and, 101–2
  in girls, 33, 117
  as symptom of abnormality
    in kidney or bladder,
    112

Vaporizer, 40, 110, 116, 127
Varicalla vaccine (VARIVAX),
  46–47
  side effects, 47
Vestibular stimulation, 68
Viral infections, 32–33
  asthma and, 115–16
  diarrhea and, 67
  ear, 62
  eye (conjunctivitis or
    pinkeye), 130
  fever and, 90
Vision problems
  lazy eye (amblyopia), 15–17

  misaligned or crossed eyes
    (strabismus), 15–16
Vocal chords: stridor, 39
Vomiting, 32–33
  excessive, 82–83

Walking, developmental
  milestones and, 60
Weight
  failure to thrive, 124–26
  loss or insufficient gain, 82,
    105
Well-baby exams
  checking hips, 54–55
  tracking motor development,
    59–60
Whooping cough (pertussis),
  88–89
  DTP shots and, 88–89

Zinc
  foods rich in, 29
  supplements, 29